ROUTLEDGE LIBRARY EDITIONS:
EXCHANGE RATE ECONOMICS

Volume 10

FOREIGN EXCHANGE AND FOREIGN DEBTS

FOREIGN EXCHANGE AND FOREIGN DEBTS

HUBERT C. WALTER

Routledge
Taylor & Francis Group
LONDON AND NEW YORK

First published in 1926 by Methuen & Co. Ltd.

This edition first published in 2017
by Routledge
2 Park Square, Milton Park, Abingdon, Oxon OX14 4RN

and by Routledge
711 Third Avenue, New York, NY 10017

Routledge is an imprint of the Taylor & Francis Group, an informa business

British Library Cataloguing in Publication Data
A catalogue record for this book is available from the British Library

ISBN: 978-0-415-79325-4 (Set)
ISBN: 978-1-315-21117-6 (Set) (ebk)
ISBN: 978-0-415-79345-2 (Volume 10) (hbk)
ISBN: 978-1-315-21101-5 (Volume 10) (ebk)

Publisher's Note
The publisher has gone to great lengths to ensure the quality of this reprint but points out that some imperfections in the original copies may be apparent.

FOREIGN EXCHANGE AND FOREIGN DEBTS

BY

HUBERT C. WALTER

M.A., LL.B. (Cantab.); F.I.S.A.

FORMERLY LECTURER IN FOREIGN EXCHANGE TO THE INSTITUTE OF BANKERS, MANCHESTER AND DISTRICT; AND LECTURER IN BANKING AND CURRENCY TO THE MUNICIPAL SCHOOL OF COMMERCE, MANCHESTER; AUTHOR OF "MODERN FOREIGN EXCHANGE."

METHUEN & CO. LTD.

36 ESSEX STREET W.C.

LONDON

First Published in 1926

PRINTED IN GREAT BRITAIN

PREFACE

MY previous textbook, "Modern Foreign Exchange," was written in 1922 from the standpoint that, as I then put it, the changes in the world of Foreign Exchange brought about by the war were "destined, in the main, to be permanent."

The correctness of this view has been amply shown by the events of the four years which have elapsed since the above was written, and the viewpoint defined in the earlier textbook is now generally held by the more far-seeing part of the business community.

During 1924 to 1925 a new set of correlated events in the world of international finance (issue of the Reichsmark, Dawes Plan, stabilization, the Return to Gold, Debt Settlements) have altered substantially the Exchange conditions of 1922. The events in question do not constitute a "return to normal" in the sense of a return to pre-war conditions—that "normal" has gone for an indefinite period. They do constitute, however, a new "normal," which is likely to last for the next few years. This new normal I have called "The New Equilibrium"; for on the one hand it is an equilibrium, which fact distinguishes it from the chaotic fluctuations of the years immediately following the war, while on the other hand it is as different from the equilibrium of pre-war days as the political state of Europe in 1926 differs from that of 1914. It is accordingly from the standpoint of this New Equilibrium that the foreign exchanges of to-day should be studied.

When, therefore, a fourth edition of "Modern Foreign Exchange" was called for in 1926, it seemed best to rewrite the whole book from the standpoint of the new conditions. The result was a new book, as was natural enough in view of the crowded happenings of the last few years in the world of Foreign Exchange. Only a part of the purely technical section of the original book, that on Bills of Exchange, preserves its original form, and even here additions have been made. The last four and a half chapters are almost entirely new.

The study of Exchange movements to-day must ultimately base itself on the new body of Exchange reasoning worked out by Professor Keynes, Professor Cassel, and others. This new body of Exchange reasoning, which explains the phenomena of Foreign Exchange as they exist to-day, has, however, still not found its way to any appreciable extent into the textbooks, which were in the main written with reference to pre-war conditions and which continue to treat modern developments, in so far as they are treated in detail at all, as temporary aberrations from pre-war conditions, which are still called "normal." The present textbook tries to explain the essentials of Exchange movements to-day as they are understood by modern economists, in a form which will be comprehensible to the intelligent person of average education who is not a professional economist. I have had in mind throughout the students and the business men of whom my original Manchester audiences were composed, to whom much of the new reasoning, which has been written by economists for economists, is complicated in form to a most discouraging degree. Accordingly, such subjects as inflation, purchasing power parity, the course of the mark, the stabilization of the Exchanges, the return to the gold standard, and international debts are discussed more fully than has hitherto been the case in textbooks, but in a less technical manner than is necessarily adopted in an economic treatise. I hope to find the justification for the book, not in original theories, but in setting out in a form which can be understood by any person of average education the agreed conclusions of economists regarding the post-war Exchanges.

Any adequate textbook on Foreign Exchange which aims at being more than a guide to the Exchange market must aim at explaining phenomena as well as describing them. The problem is to balance description and explanation, technique and theory. It must combine some of the functions of a manual on foreign banking with those of a textbook on this section of economics. Throughout I have endeavoured to bear in mind that my readers, like my audiences, will want to know not only How? but also Why?

So far as the technique of foreign banking is concerned I have, in dealing with foreign bills, drawn on my own experience of both the banking and mercantile aspects, obtained in the capacity of financial manager of a mercantile company trading in various overseas markets, which I was enabled to amplify by the facilities kindly afforded me by one of the joint-stock banks for observing the daily work of Exchange trading in its foreign branch. The section on the legal aspect of Bills of Exchange is not only essential to the understanding of why bills have come to serve as currency, but will also be helpful, it is hoped, in connexion with the whole detailed description of the practice of dealing with documentary drafts, to both the student of the law and practice of banking and the young man who is entering on a business career.

The method of presentation remains that developed by the experience of lectures delivered at the Bankers' Institute and at the Municipal School of Commerce of Manchester to audiences consisting of students preparing for the examinations of the Institute of Bankers and of business men. My obligations to existing works are numerous, and have, wherever possible, been acknowledged by footnotes. In particular, it is evident that in dealing with the effect of interest rates on the Exchanges and with Purchasing Power Parity, no textbook can escape heavy obligations to respectively the well-known works of Mr. Withers and

Professor Keynes. The short bibliography appended will, it is believed, be of assistance to students desirous of making a detailed study of particular aspects of the subject.

Finally, I am sure that the reader can best understand the Foreign Exchanges by studying their recent movements. Exchange rates do not operate in a vacuum, but in the actual world of international finance. Hence especial attention has been paid to inflation in Germany and France, deflation in Germany and Britain, price levels, foreign loans, the return to gold, and, above all, to foreign debts. It is the last-named factor which will decide the fate of the New Equilibrium and therewith the stability of existing Rates of Exchange. On no economic subject of to-day is the gulf between informed and uninformed deeper. I have attempted here to bridge that gulf by giving, for the first time so far as I am aware, a popular statement from the point of view of the Foreign Exchanges of the position created by the international debt settlements of 1925–1926. Just as the Exchange events of the half-decade following the war were determined by inflation, so those of the next few years will be determined by the debt settlements.

HUBERT C. WALTER

August 1926

CONTENTS

PART I—OUTLINES

PART II—TECHNIQUE

PART IV—THE NEW EQUILIBRIUM

FOREIGN EXCHANGE AND FOREIGN DEBTS

PART I—OUTLINES

CHAPTER I

INTRODUCTORY—CURRENCY AND GOLD

IN the spring of 1914 the present writer, who was then travelling in Germany, found the cost of living there about the same as in England. In 1922 the same journey was substantially cheaper. In 1923 it was ridiculously, fantastically cheap. In 1924 Germany was the dearest country in Europe. In 1925 the comparison was about the same as it would have been in 1913.

These wide variations of prices were due entirely to the events happening at the time in the world of foreign exchange, which caused the prices at which German marks could be bought by English pounds to vary in an astonishing manner. Similar phenomena were being reproduced all over Europe.

They, and the popular interest which they aroused, were entirely a product of the war. Before 1914 the Foreign Exchanges were of interest only to a very small number of highly-specialized dealers in the principal financial centres of the world. The great English joint-stock banks themselves put their Exchange business through these dealers. The business community cared nothing for Exchange rates. There was no reason why it should do so, for the chief Foreign Exchange rates were invariably steady; they never fluctuated by more than margins which were so very small as to be of interest only to the dealers who, in a manner that no one outside their offices understood, bar two or three students, made a living out of them.

Since the war movements in these formerly so stable rates have been violent and unexpected. So vital has been the effect of these movements on the life of the peoples concerned that Foreign Exchange rates have acquired great "news value" in Fleet Street, and have in consequence found their way on to the front pages of the newspapers. The Bankers' Institute, appreciating the altered conditions with a quickness not general in the post-war world, altered the syllabus of its examinations in 1919; previously there had only been incidental questions on Foreign Exchange in the papers on the Practice and Law of Banking. In 1920 a conference of financial experts representing most of the principal nations in Europe was held at Brussels: the report issued by these experts on existing international commercial and financial conditions centred round the unsettlement of the Exchanges. So much for the changed attitude of the financial community. In the business world the use of the phrase "collapsed exchanges" as indicative of one of the causes of the present trade depression, and of "stabilizing the exchanges" as one of the remedies for that depression, have become commonplaces: before the war both phrases were unknown to the generality of business men.

It is evident that something of a radical nature happened as a result of the war which altogether altered the working of the Foreign Exchanges; and that that alteration is having very far-reaching effects on everyday business life. Perhaps the best example of what the alteration in the exchange position means in practice is this: before the war one pound, when changed into U.S. dollars, would buy 4·86⅔ dollars' worth of wheat. During a great part of 1920 the pound would only buy 3·90 dollars' worth —about 20 per cent. less. That is equivalent to the imposition of a tax of 20 per cent. on wheat imported from the U.S.

The secret of the importance and of the complications of Foreign Exchange to-day is that all the economic forces operating in a country work themselves out in its rate of exchange. The Exchanges register the economic health of a country; to-day they register the extent to which the economic equilibrium of the world, of Europe especially, has been upset by the war.

Foreign Exchange has one quality about it which makes it both more interesting and more difficult than other sections of economics, in that it deals with economic conditions as they exist from day to day. This makes the subject more difficult, because it means the constant revising of explanations and theories. It also makes it more interesting, because we are enabled to apply our principles to the Exchanges as they exist, and check our theories accordingly.

To clarify our ideas at the outset, we may describe Foreign Exchange as the business of exchanging currencies, or as the study of the ways in which currencies are exchanged; the Foreign Exchanges are the markets in which this business is done; and Rates of Exchange are the prices of the various national currencies in terms of other national currencies.

The word "currency" is used in the same sense as the word "money" is often used. It is necessary to be clear about the meaning of these two terms. "Money" may mean a number of things, "currency" only one, There are certainly four things which the word "money" may mean:

(1) The standard or measure of value.
(2) Medium of exchange.
(3) Purchasing power.
(4) A loan of money.

The last mentioned meaning is the one in which the word is customarily used in the money articles in the newspapers. "Money was cheap to-day" or "Money was dear" obviously does not mean that twenty-one shillings could be obtained for one pound or vice versa. It simply means that if anyone wanted to borrow money, he could do so at a low or high rate of interest. There, clearly, money means "the loan of cash or credit." In the third sense of "purchasing power," an overdraft is money. In neither of these two senses is money equivalent to currency. The first two meanings quoted are in modern practice merged in each other. There is a clear enough theoretical distinction between the standard which measures value and the instrument or medium by which value is transferred from one person to another; but in the Western European industrial system the monetary system embodies both ideas. In the highly developed commercial system of ancient Babylon, the theoretical distinction was also effective in practice. In a sale of land, the price was agreed in terms of shekel-weights of silver, which were thus the standard of value, but it was paid in corn, slaves, animals, etc., which, valued on the same silver basis, served as the actual media of exchange.[1] In the Western European system to-day coins and notes serve both as standards of value and media of exchange.

Of these four meanings of the word "money," "currency" is equivalent to the second only, viz. a medium of exchange. Currency means this and only this. It has thus a much more circumscribed meaning than "money," which may have any of the other three meanings indicated. It has, however, a wider meaning than the term "Legal tender," which is that portion of the medium of exchange which a debtor can legally compel his creditor to accept in satisfaction of his debt. Thus an overdraft is money in the sense of purchasing power, but it is not currency.

[1] King: "History of Babylon," pp. 195, 196.

A cheque is currency, but not legal tender. A Treasury note is all three.

The currency of England consists of the following:

(1) Coins.
(2) Treasury notes.
(3) Bank-notes.
(4) Cheques, which are orders to bankers to pay.
(5) Bills of exchange, which are orders to pay.
(6) Interest coupons.

Of the six, the last three are what bankers call "Instruments of Credit," i.e. instruments by which credits, that is to say, book-debts, are recorded and transferred from one person to another. Such is our currency to-day. Before the war there were no Treasury notes.

The business of exchanging currencies became a necessary part of international trade as soon as international trade developed beyond the stage of barter. When we buy materials abroad, our currency has to be exchanged for the currency of the country in which the seller wishes to be paid, which is generally that of the country in which he is resident. Foreign Exchange is concerned with the quantity of our own currency which we give up in exchange for that of the seller. Assume that "A," a merchant, is trying to sell some mineral that is mined in the United States to a Dutchman. "A" knows he can get £33 per ton c.i.f. Amsterdam for the material. The price we will say is \$105 per ton at the American mine. Let us call rail freight \$5 per ton and ocean freight \$30 per ton. That gives a total cost to "A" of \$140. Pre-war, when the average rate of exchange with the United States was \$4·86 to the pound, \$140 would represent to "A" in sterling £(140 ÷ 4·86) = £28 16s., i.e. that is the sum which "A" would have had to expend in order to buy \$140 to remit to the exporter.

Assuming "A's" gross profit to be 10 per cent., he would require to sell at the price of £31 13s. 7d. In pre-war days Dutch florins could usually be bought at the rate of 12·1 florins to the pound sterling, so that the price of £31 13s. 7d., or, bringing the shillings and pence to decimals of a pound, £31·6794, would represent to prospective Dutch buyers 31·6794 × 12·1 = 383·32 florins. But if the American exchange is what it was frequently during 1919–20—$3·50 to the pound—then the amount in sterling "A" has to expend in order to purchase $140 is £(140 ÷ 3·50) = £40. Assuming the same gross profit as before (10 per cent.), "A" will now require to sell at the price of £44. Had the florin been at its usual pre-war rate of 12·1 florins to the pound sterling, this price would have represented to prospective Dutch buyers (44 × 12·1), or 532·4 florins. But at its 1920 figure of, say, 11·4 florins to the pound, £44 represents only (44 × 11·4), or 501·4 florins. Even supposing, therefore, that the mineral has remained at exactly the same price as in 1914, the price which "A" can quote to Dutch buyers has been raised from 383·32 to 501·4 florins, solely by the operation of exchange rates. Whether this increase will preclude "A" from continuing to do the business depends, *inter alia,* on whether the florin has become less valuable in terms of the dollar than it was in 1914 to the extent represented by the ratio 501·4 : 383·32. If the florin compared with the dollar has not lost in value to that extent, it will now be more advantageous to the Dutch purchaser to buy direct from New York. It is evident that fluctuations in exchange rates may, quite apart from factors of price, transport, etc., divert the currents of trade or dam them up altogether.

In the example given it will have been noticed that, at different stages of the transaction, "A" had to remit dollars to New York and the Dutch buyer had to remit sterling to London. How can remittances in foreign currency be made? In pre-war days there would have been five ways:

(1) By sending gold.

(2) By paying out of a foreign currency account.

(3) By sending interest coupons, payable in the foreign currency in question.

(4) By buying from a British bank and sending to the foreign creditor a draft in foreign currency. This draft is drawn by the British bank on a foreign bank situated in the centre in which the creditor resides—Paris, New York, Frankfort, as the case may be—and is for so many francs, dollars, or marks. A variation of this method occurs where the British bank, in return for the payment by the British debtor to it of a sum in sterling or for the authority to debit his account, instructs a bank abroad to pay to the foreign creditor a quantity of foreign currency; such instruction may be by letter (mail transfer), by telegram (telegraphic transfer), or by cable (cable transfer).

(5) By sending the foreign creditor a sterling draft, i.e. a draft entitling him to so many pounds, which he can exchange with his bank for an amount of his own currency.

No. 1 is now often impracticable, because prohibited by law; and pre-war, when it was generally permitted, it was not for obvious reasons resorted to in the ordinary way between merchants. Such sending of gold abroad as occurred was a specialized business in the hands of bullion dealers.

As to the other four of the five methods mentioned above whereby remittances abroad may be made, it will be evident that Nos. 2 and 3 are only possible in the special cases where the foreign currency account already exists or the interest coupons happen to be available.

In method No. 4, the most common method of making remittances abroad, the British bank in question has a balance in foreign currency at the foreign bank in question. In handing out a draft on that balance, or instructing the foreign bank to pay part of it away, in exchange for sterling or for the authorization to debit the customer's account, it is exchanging a foreign currency for sterling. The transaction at once raises two questions: How does the bank acquire the currency balance abroad; and at what price will it sell its draft thereon?

In method No. 5 also, where our foreign correspondent exchanges with his bank the sterling draft we sent him for a certain quantity of his own currency, two corresponding questions arise: What use will the buying bank make of the sterling draft, and at what price will it buy?

The first of each of the two questions put requires for its answer a description of the machinery of the Foreign Exchanges, a description, that is, of the means whereby foreign balances are created and remittances made out of them by the banks. The second question necessitates examining the factors which cause rates to move up and down.

CHAPTER II

MINT PARS

AS to the manner in which foreign currency balances come into existence and the manner in which they are dealt with by the banks: this will be dealt with in detail in Chapters IV and V. Here we will anticipate by saying that trading and financial transactions bring into existence such foreign balances and put them at the disposal of the banks, who in turn exchange these balances among themselves in accordance with the instructions of their customers. What we are concerned with in this and the following chapters is the rates at which the banks carry out these exchanges: at what price, that is to say, will the banks sell their foreign balances? Or to put it in another way, at what price will the banks carry out for a customer an exchange of one currency into another?

This question, which the bank's customer would put in the form, "At what price can drafts in such-and-such a currency be bought or sold?" could before the war have been very quickly answered. In those days there were fluctuations in rates, but these were very small and were definitely limited in extent. There was then never any uncertainty as to what the rates of exchange between the principal European countries and the United States would be, apart from quite minor fluctuations. The rates only moved slightly on one side or the other of a fixed point. The reason for this steadiness was that there existed an international currency, and the exchange value of the currencies of the various countries in terms of this common international currency determined their exchange value in terms of each other. This international currency was gold.[1] The use of gold as an international currency

[1] This point seems to have first been clearly made by Mr. T. Gregory. See "The Foreign Exchanges, Before, During and After the War."

determined, within narrow limits, the rates at which currencies were exchanged. The national currencies of the principal countries of Europe and Northern America each represented a certain quantity of gold: there were so many grains in the English sovereign; the mark, the dollar, the franc each represented a claim to such-and-such a fraction of a gram of gold. 25·22½ francs represented the same amount of gold as was contained in the English sovereign; therefore the pound could always be exchanged for about 25·22½ francs. The fixed point referred to above, from which the Anglo-French rate would never diverge far, was represented by the equation 25·22½ francs = £1. Similar equations obtained for all the other chief rates.

Broadly speaking, and subject to certain exceptions which will be particularized later, the claim to a certain quantity of gold which the holder of any one of these currencies possessed by virtue of holding it could be enforced in effect: if the holder went to one of the central banks and demanded gold for his currency, he could have it and do what he liked with it, including sending it out of the country. As an illustration of how easily all this worked, gold coins were in general use in all the principal European countries and North America, and it did not in the ordinary way occur to anyone to refuse to pay a debt he owed in gold through a fear that he could not get gold in turn from respectable people who owed him money.

In the case of every currency except the pound sterling there had occurred occasions when the claim to gold conferred by the possession of currency could not be enforced. These were infrequent, but when they occurred, as at the time of the U.S. banking crisis in 1907, it was just when the possessor of currency would in all probability be especially anxious to secure gold. In the case of the pound sterling, the claim to gold could always be enforced. This difference was expressed by the statement that in pre-war days London was an absolutely free market in gold, whereas the other chief financial centres, including New York, were generally, but not always, free markets in gold. In this distinction between "always" and "generally" consisted the predominance of the sterling bill and of London as the financial centre of the pre-war world.

The fact that this distinction existed should not, however, be allowed to obscure the fact that, in the ordinary way, the mark, the franc, the dollar, etc., could always be turned into gold if desired. This fact kept their value in terms of one another, i.e. their exchange value, steady: 25·22 francs were always worth about the same quantity of gold as one pound; therefore 25·22 francs could always be exchanged for approximately a pound, and vice versa. It is necessary to say "approximately," for currencies did fluctuate a little, owing to the course of trade and international borrowing; but the extent to which they could fluctuate was kept within very narrow limits by the fact that, save on very exceptional occasions, they could all be exchanged for gold without delay or difficulty.

Our exchange machinery was built up on the assumption that actual market rates could deviate only very slightly from the theoretical exchange value, which represented the gold value of the currency.

During the war exchange transactions were controlled by the warring governments in various ways which will be touched upon later.[1] Following the war, the assumption that exchange rates would fluctuate round about Mint Par, because the latter expressed the gold value of the currencies, was found to have broken down altogether, because the currencies no longer in fact possessed this gold value. They had lost it as a result of the destruction of values during the war and during the economic warfare which was carried on by the Allies after the war itself ended. By the close of 1923 the extent of the loss in value, i.e. the depreciation, which had taken place in

[1] See Chapter IX, p. 103, *et seq.*

many of the continental currencies, as compared with gold and with the U.S. dollar, was enormous. The loss in value had been accompanied by a loss in stability, and rates fluctuated in the wildest manner. Other currencies, like the pound, had by the end of 1923 passed the worst and were on the way to recovery. During 1924–1925 a new equilibrium between the rates of most of the currencies was established. This new equilibrium, which generally speaking has been maintained since, differs essentially from that which obtained in pre-war days, in that the various currencies have in general not in fact recovered their theoretical gold value, and the equilibrium is based on control by the governments or central banking authorities which aims at keeping rates in a fixed relation to gold or to the U.S. dollar. The exchange machinery does not work automatically, with occasional regulation, as before the war, but has to be unintermittently regulated. The new equilibrium is, however, based ultimately, like the pre-war equilibrium, on the theoretical gold values of the currencies, and it is accordingly by this aspect of currency matters that we have first to examine.

The theoretical gold exchange value of a currency is known by the technical term "Mint Par" or "Par of Exchange." The Mint Par or Par of Exchange is the rate at which the standard coin of one country is convertible into that of another country according to the terms of their respective mint laws. The mint laws of the principal countries of the world, apart from the East, prescribe that the standard coin of the country shall, like the sovereign, contain a certain weight of gold, or shall, like the franc, bear a fixed ratio to another coin which contains a certain weight of gold. A comparison of the weight of gold in, or represented by, the two coins, gives an equation showing that the weight of gold represented by a certain number of francs is the same as that contained in a sovereign: in other words, that number of francs equals a sovereign.

That equation is called the Mint Par between the two countries.

The Mint Par is therefore a comparison of the value of the units of two currencies on the basis, not primarily of what they will purchase, but of the amount of gold to which their possession entitles the possessor. It is a comparison of gold values.

It follows that, given the terms of the mint laws of any two gold-using countries, it is always possible to ascertain the Mint Par or Par of Exchange between them. The Mint Par between England and France may be taken as an example. The Mint regulations of the two countries are as follows:

(*a*) *England:* 480 troy ozs. of gold, $\frac{11}{12}$ths fine, shall be coined into 1,869 sovereigns.

(*b*) *France:* 1,000 gram. of gold, $\frac{9}{10}$ths fine, shall be coined into 155 napoleons, and one franc is one-twentieth of a napoleon.

We also know (*c*) that 1 oz. troy = 31·1035 gram.

Given the above data, we ascertain the Mint Par by a simple arithmetical operation. Our data we arrange in a set of simple equations, of which number (1) contains the unknown quantity of francs which will be equivalent to a sovereign, number (2) is supplied by (*a*), number (4) by (*c*) and numbers (6) and (7) by (*b*), while numbers (3) and (5) are self-evident arithmetical relations:

(1) x francs - - - = 1 sovereign.
(2) 1,869 sovereigns - = 480 troy oz. standard gold.
(3) 12 troy oz. stand. gold = 11 troy oz. fine gold.
(4) 1 troy oz. fine gold - = 31·1035 grm. fine gold.
(5) 9 grm. fine gold - = 10 grm. gold $\frac{9}{10}$ths fine.
(6) 1,000 grm. gold, $\frac{9}{10}$ths fine - - - = 155 napoleons.
(7) 1 napoleon - - = 20 francs.

Now the above columns contain two sets of items, of which every one in the left-hand column is equal to a corresponding item in the right-hand column, and vice versa. It follows that if all the items in the first column are multiplied together, the result will be equal to the product of all the items in the second column, thus:

$$x \times 1869 \times 12 \times 1 \times 9 \times 1000 \times 1 = 1 \times 480 \times 11 \times 31{\cdot}1035 \times 10 \times 155 \times 20,$$

$$\text{whence,} \quad x = \frac{480 \times 11 \times 31{\cdot}1035 \times 10 \times 155 \times 20}{1869 \times 12 \times 9 \times 1000}$$

$$= 25{\cdot}2215.$$

The Mint Par between England and France is therefore Fr. 25·2215 = £1.

This operation is—or used to be—known as the "Chain Rule." It simply consists of arranging our data in a number of simple equations, which are set out in such a way that the first denomination is the unknown quantity required, and that the first denomination of every other equation is the same as the second denomination of the equation immediately preceding it. The chain must be continued until it completes itself, i.e. until the second denomination of the last equation is the same as the first denomination of the first equation—in the case above, a certain number of francs. Then, the product of all the quantities in the first column is equal to the product of all the quantities in the second. As there is only one unknown, it can then be found by working out.

Given a knowledge of the mint laws of any two gold-using countries, the Par of Exchange between them can be found by this method.

It will be evident that there can only be a Mint Par between two countries whose standard coins are both gold. If the standard coin of one country is gold, and that of another, such as China, is silver, there can be no Mint Par between them, because there is no fixed relationship between the value of an ounce of gold and the value of an ounce of silver. There is therefore no Mint Par between London and Shanghai.

A further illustration of the meaning of Pars of Exchange is afforded by the following figures:

London/New York Par of Exchange	$4·8665 = £1.
Weight of fine gold in an English sovereign - - - - -	113·0015 troy gr.
Standard gold according to U.S. mint law - - - - -	$\frac{9}{10}$ths fine gold.

The first two lines taken together evidently mean that since each is the equivalent of the amount of gold in one gold sovereign, therefore $4·8665 must be the equivalent of 113·0015 grains of gold. Therefore the weight of fine gold in the standard coin of the United States is:

$$\frac{113{\cdot}0015}{4{\cdot}8665}\text{ troy gr.},$$

and the amount of U.S. standard gold in the standard coin must therefore be:

$$\frac{113{\cdot}0015}{4{\cdot}8665} \times \frac{10}{9},$$

or 25·8 troy gr. Such is, in fact, the provision of the American mint law. This does not mean that a gold dollar containing 25·8 troy gr. of gold $\frac{9}{10}$ths fine must be actually minted—in point of fact gold dollars have not been minted since 1890—but that "such gold coins as are struck shall contain this number of grains per dollar of their nominal or legal tender value."[1] Thus the Eagle,

[1] Whittaker, "Foreign Exchange."

one of the gold coins actually minted, has a legal tender-value of \$10; hence it must and does contain $25{\cdot}8 \times 10$ troy gr. of gold $\frac{9}{10}$ths fine.

The Mint Pars of the principal countries of the world are given in the statement of world-currencies contained in Chapter V (column two).

CHAPTER III

GOLD POINTS

THE importance of Mint Pars, which represent the theoretical exchange values of currencies based on the amount of gold represented by cash, depends on the international recognition of gold as a standard by which to measure the value of currency. If foreign exchange machinery is to work smoothly, actual rates of exchange must approximate to the Mint Par, or must at any rate stand in some definite, fixed relation to it. It is because this assumption broke down widely after the war that exchange difficulties arose which have only partly been overcome.

Before the war actual exchange rates were bound to approximate to theoretical values very closely, for the reasons given in the preceding chapter. The actual Anglo-French rate, for example, varied by only a few centimes on either side of 25·22½. Fluctuations of exchange rates on either side of Mint Par were then not only slight, but definitely limited in extent. The limits were fixed by two points called "Gold Points." These points depended upon the cost of sending gold from one country to another, and were determined respectively by adding that cost to, and subtracting it from, the Mint Par. Thus the Mint Par between London and Paris was 25·22½; assume that the cost of sending gold in either direction, inclusive of freight, packing, and insurance, was ·07 francs per sovereign; then the gold points were:

25·22½ plus ·07 = 25·29½ (upper gold point).
25·22½ minus ·07 = 25·15½ (lower gold point).

The Anglo-French Exchange would ordinarily fluctuate between 25·15½ and 25·29½, and would not, save in extra-ordinary cases, move outside those limits.

The statement that the limits within which the rates of exchange would fluctuate were fixed by adding to, and subtracting from, the Mint Par the cost of shipping gold is known as the "Gold Point Theory." As such we shall refer to it; but it is necessary to bear in mind that it was not only a theory, but also a description of what actually happened in practice, subject to certain modifications, which we shall consider later.

Why the cost of shipping gold should fix the limits of exchange fluctuations is not difficult to understand. Suppose "A," an Englishman, having a debt to pay in Paris, went to his bankers and asked them for a draft in francs on Paris. He expected they would sell him a draft on a Parisian bank, with whom they kept their balances in francs. The bankers offered to sell him a draft at the rate of 25·14 francs to the pound. "A" would not accept that, because he could send gold more cheaply. The cost of sending gold to Paris, including the charges of the bullion dealer who attended to the shipment, insurance, and freight, was, say, ·07 francs. When the gold arrived at Paris it would realize 25·22 francs for every sovereign. The whole transaction cost "A" seven centimes for every sovereign, so that the nett quantity of francs obtained for every sovereign sent was 25·15. By buying a draft from his banker "A" would have obtained only 25·14 francs. Obviously it was more advantageous to "A" to get 25·15 francs for his sovereign than 25·14 francs. It paid him better therefore to send gold than to buy a draft from his bankers.

Now, assume that "B" in Paris had to pay money in London. His bankers asked, for a draft in sterling, 25·30 francs for every pound. For "B" it was cheaper to send gold. When the gold arrived at London it would realize one pound for every 25·22 francs' worth. It had cost the Frenchman to get the gold over here ·07 francs for every 25·22 francs, so that he had in fact remitted the money to London at the rate of 25·29 francs per pound, which was evidently more advantageous to him than buying a sterling draft at 25·30 francs per pound.

Assuming then, that the cost of sending gold from London to Paris remained constant at 7 centimes per sovereign, gold would be shipped from London to Paris when the rate tended to go below 25·15, and from Paris to London when it tended to go above 25·29. In point of fact, bullion dealers and Foreign Exchange dealers in London and Paris respectively would, when the exchange reached these points, ship gold themselves, and thereby create for themselves balances in the other centre against which they would draw drafts. The fact that this would be done prevented the market rates quoted from going below 25·15 or above 25·29. If the cost of sending gold became less, then the gold points drew a little nearer to one another; if the cost of sending gold became more, then the points moved away from each other. The limits of the fluctuations of exchange were definitely fixed by adding to or subtracting from the Mint Par the cost of shipping gold.

The Gold Point Theory was before the war not only a theory but a description of the relations which actually obtained between the chief gold-using centres of the world. There were, however, certain exceptions of detail, relating to both the upper and lower gold points. As regards the lower, gold used on occasion to leave England before, according to the theory, it should have done. The reasons for this are matters of detail which are now of purely historical interest.[1] As regards the upper gold point, rates used on occasion to reach, and pass, the upper gold point without gold coming in. The reason in such a case was that it might be prevented from leaving other countries, as mentioned in Chapter II. London was the only financial centre in the world where no hindrance, legal or

[1] They are examined in detail in Withers' "Money-Changing," pp. 161–2.

practical, was ever placed in the way of the outflow of gold. In Paris, in New York, and Berlin, it was on certain occasions impossible for would-be shippers to obtain gold.

With these modifications the Gold Point Theory held good in practice. That is what is meant by the statement that before the war international indebtedness could always be settled by the shipment of gold. That is not of course to say that the exchanges were normally corrected by this means. Normally, indeed, before the war, the corrective to exchange movements was supplied by the ordinary processes of trade [1] or by the manipulation of discount rates.[2] The operation of these two factors we shall discuss in detail later. The importance of shipments of gold lay in this, that where trade processes or manipulation of discount rates failed to correct the fluctuations of the exchanges, shipments of gold were always a possibility in reserve. They were not normally required in order to fix the exchanges between the gold points, but where the two factors named were not adequate to effect this, there was always the possibility of shipping gold, and that possibility was used on a number of occasions. The exchanges before the war never reached a point at which the rates were too far from the Mint Par to be corrected by the shipment of gold.

Gold was thus an international currency, and the assumptions were justified that a country's currency was a claim to so much gold, and that that claim could if desired be enforced. In other words, if an Englishman had a draft payable in Berlin or Frankfort in marks, or in Paris in francs, that draft represented a claim to so much gold from Germany or France as the case might be. If a Frenchman had a draft payable in London in sterling, that draft represented a claim to so much gold from England. In either case the claim could be enforced if desired. These are the assumptions underlying the Gold Point Theory.

[1] Examined in Chapters VIII and IX. [2] Examined in Chapter XI.

Both assumptions are only partially true to-day. Entirely different conditions came into existence as a result of the war. Each of the belligerent countries, with the exception of the United States, issued an amount of paper currency far in excess of its gold cover. In addition to these large issues of paper money which could not be converted into gold, substantial debts had been incurred by the various States to their members in the form of short-term obligations, i.e. promises to pay which matured at the expiration of a short period, like our own Floating Debt; and further large debts were owing by the continental belligerents to Britain and by the same debtors and Britain to the U.S. The first of these effects of the war, the issue of large quantities of paper which was not convertible into the gold which it nominally represented caused the value of the currencies in question to depreciate in value in terms of gold and of those currencies which retained their full value, like the U.S. dollar, or which nearly retained it, like the Swedish krone and the Dutch florin. The pound depreciated in this way to some extent and the continental currencies very much more. Such large masses of paper money were issued that the possession of these currencies could not in practice entitle the possessor to the equivalent in gold—there was not enough gold to cover the amount of currency issued. In England paper money was over-issued, and the process went to its extreme extent in Russia, Poland, Austria, and Germany. The contracting of larger internal and external debts made the loss in value still greater, for reasons which will appear later. Some of the countries in question then, in 1924–1925, issued new currencies which, except in the case of Poland, have so far been limited by the extent of their cover in gold or in foreign currencies equivalent to it, thereby restoring in these cases the truth of the first assumption of the Gold Point hypothesis, while Britain managed to restore her currency to its nominal gold value. The means whereby the results were brought about will be explained in detail later; here we are only concerned to sum up results in order to obtain a general view of the extent to which the assumptions on which the Gold Point theory is based, or, to put it more accurately, the conditions under which the Gold Point hypothesis holds good, do in fact exist to-day. The first of these conditions, then, the maintenance of the theoretical gold value of the currencies, has been in large part restored, as in the countries referred to, while in the United States it was never violated. In other countries, however, of which France is the chief, the currency at present in issue still[1] remains far below its nominal gold value. To sum up, the first assumption of the Gold Point hypothesis, that currency represents a claim to a certain quantity of gold, has been generally, but by no means universally, restored, but in its restored form it is subject to a limitation which did not exist before the war: to the limitation, viz., that the quantity of gold in question is frequently less than the quantity provided for in the Mint Laws of the country in question.

As regards the second assumption which underlies the Gold Point hypothesis—that the claim to gold can be enforced—this was entirely destroyed during the war and is now only restored very partially. The prohibitions generally imposed during the war on the export of gold were continued after it ended and are still generally in force in Europe to-day, save in certain countries where they were lifted in 1925: these countries are Britain, Holland, Sweden, the Union of South Africa, Australia, and New Zealand. There has not been since the end of the war any such prohibition in the United States. Elsewhere the prohibition still generally exists, frequently in law and certainly in fact.

The result of the failure during the post-war years of the two assumptions on which the Gold Point hypothesis

[1] June, 1926.

exists and of their partial and limited restoration in 1924–1925 is that the Gold Point hypothesis is to-day in operation only as between the countries just named. Thus it is in operation between Britain, where the assumptions have been restored in full, and the United States, where they never failed, but not between Britain and France, where the currency does not represent any fixed and definite quantity of gold; or between Great Britain and Germany, where the export of gold is forbidden unless expressly permitted by the financial authorities.

The breaking down of the assumptions on which the Gold Point hypothesis rested was thus the result of the war and of the events which followed it. During the war exchange rates had been maintained in a state of suspended animation, functioning sporadically as they were operated on by the warring governments. Between 1918 and 1924–1925, in which latter years the conditions necessary to the working of the Gold Point hypothesis were partially restored, the currencies of Europe lost in greater or less degree all relation to their Mint Par value, and exchange rates fluctuated wildly. Having ceased to represent definite quantities of gold, the currencies in question lost their intrinsic value, that is, the value which before the war they possessed in themselves by virtue of being a claim to so much gold. Currency always had value in another sense: in the sense that it was purchasing power. If a man had so many marks at his disposal, they always had value in the sense that if he went into a shop in Berlin he could buy a certain quantity of goods. But apart from that, these marks had a value in themselves because they represented so much gold. That is what is meant by intrinsic value. When, through over-issue of paper notes, a currency lost its intrinsic value, its exchange price came to depend on this other value, its value as purchasing power.

In losing intrinsic value, currencies also lost stability, because their value, being merely what they can purchase, fluctuated from day to day. At a time when prices are rising or falling rapidly, owing to alterations in the price of raw material, wages, etc., the value of a currency which represents solely purchasing power fluctuates accordingly. Currencies came to represent merely a right to a fluctuating quantity of the produce of the country in question, and nothing more.

Having lost the gold basis, and with it intrinsic value and stability, the currencies in question were at the mercy of market conditions. Extreme cases of this were seen in Eastern and Central Europe, where some currencies lost value altogether. German notes, for example, became literally worthless. Hawkers in the Strand sold notes of the nominal value of milliards[1] of marks, i.e. of a theoretical value of millions of pounds, for twopence each, at which price they were grossly overvalued; Austrian krone notes were used as labels for soda-water bottles.

As the exchange rates of these ruined currencies went down, prices expressed in terms of them went up; it was the wild and sudden fluctuations in exchange rates which caused the greatest difficulties. What the loss of stability in currency values means in practice can easily be seen. Assume that a German importer buys a quantity of raw material through a London merchant, and has to pay in sterling. The price, let us say, is £240, payable by a three months' bill. The rate of exchange at the time the purchase is made is Mk. 800. The cost of raw material he accordingly reckons at Mk. 240 × 800 = Mk. 192,000, which sum he will have to pay at the end of three months. Assuming that the work put into the raw material costs him, including all charges, an amount equal to the cost of raw material, then his final cost will be Mk. 192,000 × 2 = Mk. 384,000. If he contents himself with 5 per cent. profit, his selling price will be Mk. 403,200. By the time the bill is due, however, the value of the mark has fallen,

[1] One milliard = one thousand millions.

and the rate is no longer 800 but 1,200. The transaction then appears as follows:

Marks required to pay bill of £240 = 240 × 1200 Mk. - - -	= Mk. 288,000
Marks expended in labour and charges -	192,000
Total Cost - - - -	480,000
Sale Price - - - -	403,200
Loss - -	Mk. 76,800

In other words, a perfectly sound business transaction has been turned into a loss by the mere operation of exchange forces over which the importer had no control. It can easily be understood how under these conditions the most legitimate trade may become nothing more than a gamble.

In view of the course of the mark in the autumn of 1921 and summer of 1922 the fluctuation assumed above is a very moderate one—no more, in fact, than actually happened on occasion during a single week-end.

As the Gold Point hypothesis no longer applies generally, currencies are at the mercy of market conditions, save in so far as these can be controlled by measures taken by government and central banking authorities. The study of exchange fluctuations to-day is therefore much wider than in pre-war days. Then it was mainly a question of under what conditions would rates move to the fractional percentages which would lead to gold shipments. Now it is a question of the influence exerted on exchange movements by the financial, economic, and political conditions obtaining in the countries concerned. With these issues the last and largest section of this book will be concerned.

Before, however, these issues can usefully be examined, before, that is, we examine how the exchange machinery works, it is clearly necessary to examine the structure of that machinery itself. We come, then, to the first of the questions asked at the close of Chapter I: How do balances in foreign currency come into existence, and what use is made of them, and by whom?

PART II—TECHNIQUE

CHAPTER IV

BILLS OF EXCHANGE

STARTING from the beginning, we may take the case where the foreign department of the Manchester office of one of the joint-stock banks sells to a customer a draft on a foreign country—let us say a draft in kroner on a bank in Stockholm. A number of customers will come in and ask for such drafts, and the bank's balance in Swedish kroner in Stockholm will become exhausted unless replenished. To replenish that balance the branch applies to its head office in London. The London office buys the necessary kroner from a foreign exchange broker who specializes in Swedish exchange. But that only removes the question further back. How does the broker get possession of the kroner? The answer is, in outline, that the broker buys debts owing by Swedes to English merchants, and sells them to the foreign department of the head office. These debts are in the form of bills of exchange. What the broker does is to buy bills of exchange drawn on, i.e. payable by, people in Stockholm, and sell them to the head office of the bank. The price at which the broker sells will ultimately be determined by the price at which he can buy; the price at which he can buy will be determined by the demand and the quantities there are on offer. The price at which he sells to the London bank will determine the price at which the head office of that bank will sell the kroner to its branches, and that in turn will determine the price at which the branches will sell kroner to their customers who want drafts. Ultimately, therefore, the price at which a draft on Stockholm can be sold depends upon the price at which the bills of exchange on Stockholm can be bought. It is bills of exchange which provide the funds on which foreign drafts are drawn. The international indebtedness with which foreign exchange deals is made up of claims which in the main take the form of, or are settled by the remittance of, bills. The price of a foreign currency is the price of bills drawn on that foreign centre. It goes to the very core of the subject, therefore, to examine bills in detail. What are bills of exchange and how do they originate?

Suppose H.C.W. & Co., Ltd., are merchants importing timber from the Baltic provinces. They have to pay fairly prompt cash for the timber they import. Their customers are, in the main, builders, notoriously slow payers. H.C.W. & Co., Ltd., will in a number of cases draw bills on them, which take the form of orders to them to pay at a certain time.

The bill of exchange is in the following form:

No....... £100 0s. 0d. Date......
At ninety days' date pay to our order the sum of one hundred pounds. Value received.

For and on behalf of
H.C.W. & Co., Ltd.,
To Messrs. A. & B., Ltd., T. Brown, Secretary.
Salisbury.

This document, with invoice and delivery note for the timber, is sent to Messrs. A. & B., Ltd., or the documents may be presented through a bank. A. & B. keep the delivery note and get the timber, and return the bill, having written across the face of it:

Accepted. Date...... Payable at Barclays Bank, Salisbury.
For and on behalf of A. & B., Ltd.,
J. Jones, Secretary.

H.C.W. & Co., Ltd., can now sell this document to a bank for cash, with which they can pay for the timber imported. The price the banker will pay for it will be something less than the face value of £100; it will be £100 less interest for the period the bill has to run calculated at the rate obtaining for that class of bill. Ninety-three days after the date of the bill the then holders of the bill will present it to Barclays Bank, Salisbury, who will pay it and debit the A. & B. Co.'s account.

In this case the bill was in the first instance merely evidence of a debt which A. & B. owe H.C.W. & Co.; when sold to the banker it became an Instrument of Credit, a means, i.e. whereby A. & B.'s debt was transferred from H.C.W. & Co., Ltd., to the banker. The banker who has bought it may in turn sell it to a broker, he to a fourth buyer. In thus going from hand to hand it is serving as currency in the same way as a Treasury note.

These bills of exchange have been well-known commercial instruments since the fourteenth century. They were developed first among the Italian commercial community in Florence, where banking originated. From Italy they spread through the commercial cities of Germany—the Rhineland towns and the Hansa League—to England. During the following centuries they came more and more into use among merchants, but the rights and obligations of the parties to them were not recognized by the common law. Such was the position at the beginning of the nineteenth century. The law is built up largely on decided cases. During the first quarter of the nineteenth century a large body of commercial customs, which previously had not had the force of law, became incorporated into the English common law through the decisions of a number of Lord Chancellors, more particularly of Lord Eldon; and among such commercial customs were a number relating to bills of exchange. From time to time conflicting decisions were given, which created difficulties for the commercial community. Towards the end of the century a portion of the commercial law of this country was codified, one portion so treated being the whole of the law relating to bills of exchange and cheques, which is now to be found in the Bills of Exchange Act of 1882.

By that act a bill of exchange is defined as " an unconditional order in writing, addressed by one person to another, signed by the person giving it, requiring the person to whom it is addressed to pay on demand or at a fixed determinable future time a certain sum in money to or to the order of a specified person or to bearer." In other words, it is an order from " A " to " B " to pay a certain sum at a determinable time to " A " or to " C." The amount and the time must both be definite.

The following details regarding the form in which bills are drawn, and the rights and liabilities of parties to them, are material.

In the example quoted, H.C.W. & Co., Ltd., are the drawers of the bill, and A. & B., Ltd., are the drawees. As the bill is payable to the order of H.C.W. & Co., Ltd., the latter are also the payees, but the payees might equally well have been a third party, such as a bank, who were collecting the bill on behalf of H.C.W. & Co., Ltd. In the case given, when A. & B., Ltd. promised to pay, or, in other words " accepted," the bill by writing that word across the face of it, they became acceptors. Save in exceptional circumstances, a bill can only be accepted by the drawee. The acceptance, again, might simply have read :

Accepted
For and on behalf of A. & B., Ltd.,
J. Jones, Secretary.

Such an acceptance is known as an " Acceptance in Blank."

There is one other party to a bill who requires mention, and that is the endorser. When " X " sells a bill, accepted by " K," " X " will write his name on the back, thereby becoming an endorser. The acceptor " K " is primarily liable on the bill, but if " K " fails to pay the bill when it is due, the holder can sue either " K," or " X " (or any other endorser), or the drawer. If the holder recovers from " X," " X " in turn can recover from any previous endorser, or from " K," or from the drawer.

A bill may be drawn at sight, in which case it has to be paid as soon as it is presented, and is known as a " Sight Draft." Bills may also be drawn at 8, 30, 60, or 90 days' sight or date, or longer. If the bill is claused " At thirty days' sight pay . . .," the period runs from the date when the bill was sighted, i.e. presented, for acceptance; if it is claused " At thirty days' date pay . . .," the period runs from the date of the bill itself, irrespective of when it was sighted. In the case of both bills drawn at so many days' sight and so many days' date the period is increased by three days of grace, so that a bill at 30 days' sight is in fact payable 33 days after sight, a bill at 60 days' date at 63 days after date. But the date must be a definite, ascertained date; not some indetermined time, such as " when delivery of the goods is made." The date on which a bill becomes due for payment is known as " maturity."

If a bill is payable on demand by a banker it is called a cheque; if it is payable forthwith or at any future time by anyone else than a banker, or payable in the future by a banker, it is a bill of exchange in the ordinary sense. In other words, the phrase " Bill of Exchange " is a little vague in meaning. Legally it means all documents which come within the definition quoted above.[1] In practice, we abstract a certain class of such documents and call them " cheques." The class so abstracted consists of those bills which are payable by a banker on demand. This is equivalent to saying a cheque is a sight draft drawn on a banker. The money columns of the newspapers, however,

[1] See p. 29.

frequently use the term " cheque " for any sight draft : thus the term " the Paris cheque " means a sight draft on Paris.

A sight draft has only a 2d. stamp, whereas a bill of exchange of any other kind has to be stamped *ad valorem*, at the following rates :

Up to £25	- - - 3d.
£25 to £50	- - - 6d.
£50 to £75	- - - 9d.
£55 to £100	- - - 1s.
£100 to £200	- - - 2s.,
etc., etc.	

Two other terms should be noted : " Trade Paper " and " Bank Paper." Trade paper consists of bills accepted by merchants. Bank paper means bills accepted by banking institutions. The words " banking institution " is used advisedly to indicate not merely the joint-stock banks, but any of the merchant banks or accepting houses. A merchant bank or accepting house is a banking institution which specializes in commercial credit operations. It receives commission for lending its credit. It does this by allowing approved clients, usually merchants, to draw bills on it up to a specified amount, not relating to any particular shipment of goods, and sometimes not to any goods at all. The merchant who draws such drafts discounts them with his own bank and thus provides himself with ready cash. When drawing he obligates himself to put the accepting house in funds to meet the draft 48 hours before it is due for acceptance. He pays the acceptors a commission ($\frac{3}{8}$ per cent. to $\frac{5}{8}$ per cent.) immediately the draft is returned to him accepted, and also pays the acceptors' expenses in respect of postage. By the time the bill matures—such drafts are usually of two or three months' maturity—the merchant has received the payments he was anticipating and remits the value of the draft to the accepting house 48 hours before it is due to be presented to the latter for payment.

A draft not relating to any goods at all is known as a "Finance Bill," as opposed to a "Commercial Bill," and the drawer is said to be drawing against a blank credit. For some time past the Bank of England is understood to have expressed some doubt as to the wisdom of giving blank credits, and a new form of bill has come into existence which is a hybrid between a commercial bill, which relates to a shipment of foods, and a finance bill proper, which is drawn under a blank credit and does not relate to any goods at all. This hybrid bill is drawn against a blank credit, as is the finance bill proper, but is secured by the merchant giving to the accepting house a general lien on all his shipments, or on all his shipments to a particular market,[1] and on the proceeds arising therefrom, which proceeds he agrees to place in a separate account earmarked for the purpose of repaying the loan from the acceptors. Under these arrangements between merchants and accepting houses it is frequently provided that a merchant is at liberty to draw up to a certain amount, say £10,000, and that when any part of the £10,000 is repaid by him he may immediately draw that amount again, thereby bringing up the total of the advances to him to £10,000 again. A continuing credit of this kind is known as a "revolving credit."

Such being the general character and the uses of bills of exchange, we have now to examine how it is that these documents can serve, not merely as evidence of debts and as instruments of credit, but as currency. They are enabled to do this by the possession of certain legal characteristics which make bills of exchange documents of a class known as "negotiable instruments." The chief of these characteristics of bills of exchange are two :

(*a*) They are transferable by delivery.
(*b*) Delivery gives a good title.

The quality of being transferable by delivery may be

[1] A Specimen Letter of Lien is given in Appendix to this Chapter.

thus explained. If a person is selling shares, he has to sell them by means of a document in a particular form, known as a "Transfer." Unless the sale is made by means of a transfer it is not valid. In the case of a bill of exchange no such document is needed. A good legal sale is effected by "A" handing to "B" the money, and "B" endorsing the bill and handing it to "A." That is known as "delivery," and delivery alone effects a sale. There is no need for a transfer form such as is necessary in the case of a share certificate.

As regards (*b*), "Delivery gives a good title." Suppose "A" loses a watch, "B" finds it and sells it to "C." "C" does not know that "B" is not the owner of the watch, and pays a fair price for it. It comes to "A's" knowledge that "C" has his watch. "A" can compel "C" to return it to him. "A" could sue "C" if necessary and the Court would give "A" the watch. "C" has no good title to the watch, although he bought it *bona fide* and for value. Now suppose "A" has a bill of exchange which "B" steals and sells to "C." "C" does not know that "B" has got the bill wrongly, and buys it in good faith, paying a good price for it. "A" has no right of action against "C." "C" has a good title to the bill as against "A." Although "B" himself had no title to the bill, he can give a title to "C." A party in "C's" position who has bought the bill of exchange for value, and *bona fide*, unaware that "B" had no good title to the bill, is called the "Holder in Due Course."

To be a Negotiable Instrument a document must possess both characteristics (*a*) and (*b*), as does, e.g., a banknote or Treasury note. A bill of lading is (*a*) transferable by delivery, like a bill of exchange ; but it is not (*b*) capable of acquiring a good title by delivery, and therefore it is not a negotiable instrument. The ordinary cheque, which is simply a particular form of a bill of exchange, possesses (*a*) and (*b*) and is therefore negotiable. The effect of crossing a cheque "not negotiable" does not, and is not intended to,

3

prevent or restrict transfer of the cheque by ordinary endorsement; the effect of such crossing is that the person receiving the cheque gets no better title than had the person from whom he obtains it. Crossing a cheque "not negotiable," in other words, leaves characteristic (*a*) untouched but destroys (*b*).

The bill of exchange owes its ability to serve as currency first to its legal character as a negotiable instrument, and secondly to its common commercial use. A Foreign Bond transferable by delivery is equally a negotiable instrument, but it does not serve as currency, because it does not possess the commercial popularity of the bill of exchange.

Bills of exchange serve as currency by being transferred from one to another by sale, a process which is known as "discounting" or "negotiating." When H.C.W. & Co., Ltd., negotiated the bill accepted by the A. & B. Co., Ltd., with H.C.W. & Co.'s bankers, the latter, we saw, paid the H.C.W. & Co., Ltd., a price which was the face value of the bill less an amount representing interest for the period the bill had to run. The interest is known as discount. The price of a bill is quoted in terms of the rate of discount which will be deducted from it. In this case it was a three months' bill, and on the particular date in question three months' Trade Bills were quoted in the Press at, say, $5\frac{1}{2}$ per cent. A "Trade Bill" is one which, like the bill under discusison, is drawn on and accepted by a trading firm, that is, any firm not a bank. The quotation means that trade bills which have three months to run can be sold at a price which is arrived at by deducting interest at $5\frac{1}{2}$ per cent. for the period which the bill has to run. The amount therefore which the H.C.W. & Co., Ltd., will get for their bill of £100 is arrived at as follows:

$$\text{£}100 \text{ minus } \frac{100 \times 11 \times 1}{100 \times 2 \times 4} = \text{£}100 \text{ minus } 1\tfrac{3}{8}$$
$$= \text{£}100 \text{ minus £}1\ 7\text{s. }6\text{d.}$$
$$= \text{£}98\ 12\text{s. }6\text{d.}$$

The specimen bill set out above was an inland bill. A foreign bill is one drawn or payable in a foreign centre. It is with foreign bills that we are mainly concerned. They are more complicated than inland bills, and the procedure followed in dealing with them is varied. At a later stage we shall have to deal with foreign bills exhaustively, but here we are only concerned with their use as currency and their function in building up foreign currency balances on which banks can draw drafts. We will therefore examine, in outline only, two ways in which foreign bills come into existence and create foreign balances, remembering meantime that there are alternative ways of dealing with them to those we are assuming.

Suppose " X " is a firm exporting structional steelwork to Swedish contractors known as Franssons. " X " has an agent in Stockholm. " X " ships the steelwork and sends the invoice and shipping documents to his agent, together with a 60 days' draft on Franssons for 1,000 kr. The agent gets Franssons' acceptance of the draft and thereupon hands them the shipping documents giving control of the goods. The accepted bill, we will assume, is returned to " X " in about ten days. A bill-broker, i.e. a dealer in bills, who specializes in Swedish Exchange, buys the draft from " X " and sells it to the Foreign Department of a London bank. The later send it to their Swedish correspondents to await maturity, when it will be paid and credited to the London bank's account. From the time when the bank buys the draft, it is in a position to draw drafts on its Swedish correspondents of such a maturity that they will fall due for payment coincidently with the crediting of their account with the proceeds of the draft on Franssons. Or the Swedish correspondents might be requested to discount the draft themselves and place the proceeds to the credit of the London bank's account, and do so, whereupon the London bank would be able to draw sight drafts at once.

The bill might be dealt with in another way. The agent having got it accepted might sell it to a Swedish bank, and remit to " X " that bank's draft in kroner. In that case " X " could sell the kroner draft to the bill-broker, and the same result is achieved.

Yet another possibility is that " X " might send the draft for collection. In that case " X " would take it to his own bank and ask them to collect. His bank would send the draft and documents with it to their branch or correspondents in Stockholm. The latter would present the draft for acceptance, and when it was accepted would hand over the documents just as the agent had done. When the draft matured, in one or two months, they would present it again for payment. When it was paid they would advise and credit " X's " bank here and the latter would credit " X " with the equivalent in sterling. " X's " bank now has a balance in kroner in Stockholm, and can draw on that kroner balance which it acquired by collecting " X's " bill, and sell the drafts once again to our bill-broker.

The bill drawn on Franssons has thus illustrated how a foreign bill operates to replenish the kroner balances of a British bank.

Had the bill been drawn, not in kroner, but in sterling the question would have arisen, when Franssons paid: At what rate would they pay kroner for each pound of the face value of the bill? That question we must leave until later.[1] The point we are concerned with is that Franssons would have had to pay kroner, so that whether the draft is drawn in sterling or kroner it would have the same effect of putting a bank here in possession of a kroner balance in Stockholm, against which they can issue drafts; and that it would be at their own discretion whether such drafts were issued at sight or at so many days' date or sight.

The example given is the sort of thing which, in general

[1] See Chapter VI.

outline, is happening every day. Every day there are drafts moving about for different amounts, in different currencies, on different financial centres, and maturing at different dates. The bill-broker buys the drafts he knows the banks will want, and sells to the banks which want them. The price at which the bill-broker sells the drafts to the banks will determine the price at which the Foreign Department of the banks will sell to their branches, and that price will in turn determine the price at which the branches will sell to their customers. The price at which the bill-broker sells will in turn be determined by the price at which he can buy. Therefore the price at which drafts on a foreign centre can be sold to customers at any given time will be determined by the price at which bills on that centre can be bought. That price in turn will depend on the supply of and the demand for bills, actual and anticipated.

As to the supply, it is evident from the above example that bills on Stockholm will come into existance as a result of exports to Sweden. The more goods we export to Sweden the bigger will be the kroner balance on which banks here can draw, and assuming that the demand for kroner remains the same, there will be more kroner available than there would have been if " X " and other merchants had not sold goods to Sweden, and thereby created the balance. The demand for kroner being unaltered, and the supply having increased, the value will go down. In other words, buyers of kroner will get more kroner for every pound than they got before. The exchange rate will go up: the value of sterling, in terms of kroner, has increased. We come to the conclusion that, all other things being equal, exports will send up the value of a country's currency.

Now as to the demand for bills on Stockholm. Suppose " Y " to be a merchant importing paper. " Y " will want to buy kroner drafts to pay for his imports. Every shipment of paper to this country will give rise to a demand from " Y " and similar merchants, or from their banks, for kroner bills, with which to replenish their Swedish balances. Assuming the supply of kroner remains unaltered, and this increased demand, the value of kroner will go up. For every point " Y " or his bank will get less kroner than previously. The exchange rate will go down: the value of sterling, in terms of kroner, has declined. Therefore, other things being equal, a surplus of imports over exports will tend to diminish the value of a country's currency, just as a surplus of exports over imports will tend to increase it.

The bill on Stockholm came into existence as the result of the export of goods to Sweden, and the bill on London as the result of the import of goods into England. But bills on London may come into existence as the result of the shipment of goods from one part of the world direct to another without coming to England. London in effect pays for, or guarantees the payment for, the goods to the seller and collects the price from the buyer, plus a commission for the trouble and the responsibility taken. London finances international trade and takes a tribute therefrom for doing so, and the process brings bills on London into existence and creates a corresponding demand for sterling. An example will make this clear.

A Chinaman, Chung Ling Soo, in Canton, exports tea. An Italian merchant, Valentini, in Milan, imports tea. Valentini wishes to place a contract with Chung Ling Soo for tea. Chung Ling Soo is willing to sell to Valentini, provided terms of payment can be arranged to mutual satisfaction, the difficulty being that while both persons are of undoubted financial rectitude, they are unknown to each other, and therefore not prepared to trust each other. Valentini does not wish to pay for the tea until it arrives at the Italian port, and Chung Ling Soo does not want to ship the tea until he is paid, or knows for certain that he will be paid. The gulf is bridged by an accepting house. Steinfelds are, let us say, an accepting house in London. Their business is lending their credit for a consideration.

What they do in this case is to agree to pay the bills for Valentini up to a certain amount, the consideration being that Valentini is to put them in funds to the amount of the bills at least 48 hours before they mature in London, and to pay them a commission for taking the responsibility as against Chung Ling Soo. Steinfelds, therefore, get a commission and two days' interest on the money of someone else, and that without the outlay of a penny. Steinfelds informs the London office or agents of the Canton Bank that they (Steinfelds) will accept bills drawn by Chung Ling Soo on themselves, at, let us say, 60 days, covering the shipment of tea to Valentini at a certain price. Steinfelds take the risk which Chung Ling Soo will not take, because Chung Ling Soo is simply a tea merchant, while Steinfelds are an accepting house, and it is part of their business to know on behalf of whom they can safely accept bills, and on behalf of whom they cannot. Chung Ling Soo on his part is quite prepared to take Steinfeld's assurance of payment, where he would not take Valentini's, because, as a merchant, he knows the repute of Steinfelds.

Chung Ling Soo ships the tea, and draws on Steinfelds. He presents the bill on Steinfelds together with documents covering the shipment to the Canton Bank, and the Canton manager of that bank is ready to advance him money on the bill drawn on Steinfelds although it is not yet accepted, because Steinfelds have promised that they will accept. Steinfelds' reputation is such that the promise is good enough for the manager in Canton. He sends the bill, together with documents, to his head office in London. The London office present to Steinfelds, Steinfelds accept, and when it falls due 60 days after sight they pay. In return for accepting they get the documents covering the tea, which is now on its way. How Steinfelds deal with the documents is a matter of detail. Valentini may be an old and valued client, and they may be willing to send him the documents straight away and simply ask him to remit before the draft matures. His remittance will most likely take the form of a sight draft on a London banker, which he will buy from his banker. It may be that they will draw on Valentini, and send their draft, with the documents covering the tea, to a bank in Milan, the documents to be handed over against acceptance or against payment of their draft. The important point is that they send the documents to him and he pays them, either by buying a bill on London, or by paying their draft on him, at least 48 hours before the draft on him matures.

In this transaction there is first the coming into existence of a bill on London and then the buying of a bill on London or alternately the drawing of a bill on Milan. Chung Ling Soo drew on Steinfelds; Valentini, in order to meet his financial obligations, buys a bill on London or accepted one on himself. Both these operations have arisen out of a shipment of tea from Canton to Milan, which does not come to England at all.

Balancing the transaction, it is evident that London has paid away so much and has got in rather more, the difference being represented by Steinfelds' commission and the 48 hours' interest. That is an example of how London finances world trade, and takes a commission for doing so, the process being operated by two bills, one on London and one on Milan. The whole operation clearly hinges on the willingness of Chung Ling Soo to accept without question payment by a bill on London. That willingness originated in the fact that before the war a bill on London was the safest form of international currency, because it was equivalent to a claim to so much gold, and that claim could be enforced with a certainty which did not quite apply in the case of a similar bill on New York, Paris, or Berlin. The value of a bill on London in terms of other currencies could not vary beyond the minute fluctuations which would bring it to the gold points. To-day a bill on New York from a purely currency point of view would be as good, because a bill on New York is equally a claim to gold. In fact, the financing of world trade by dollar bills has increased greatly since the war for this reason, and is likely to continue to do so in the future.[1] At the present time, both the sterling and the dollar bills are used as international currency.

Referring now to what was said earlier in this chapter regarding finance bills, it will be evident that foreign as well as English merchants can and do avail themselves of the facilities offered by the London accepting houses ; and that where a foreign merchant has drawn against a Revolving Credit he will have, before the maturity of the bill, to buy sterling and remit it to the acceptors. He will also have to pay the acceptance commission in sterling. The acceptance business, therefore, as well as ordinary trading operations, will bring bills on London into existence and create corresponding and slightly larger demands for sterling.

To sum up the conclusions of the latter part of this chapter :

(1) Ordinary trade bills come into existence as the result of the export and import of goods.

(2) Bills on London, and corresponding demands for sterling, come into existence as the result of shipments of goods from one part of the world direct to another, without coming to London.

(3) Other things being equal, a surplus of exports over imports will raise the value of a country's currency, and a surplus of imports over exports will lower it.

(4) To avoid misconception, it should be added that there are other factors than imports and exports of goods which will create a demand for and a supply of bills ; and that the value, in relation to gold, of the currency of the country on which the bills are drawn is also an important

[1] See Chapter XVIII for a brief comparison of London and New York as financial centres.

element in their price. These matters will be examined in detail later.

(5) The credit facilities supplied by London bring finance bills on London into existence; and if these are drawn abroad there will be a corresponding and slightly larger demand for sterling from abroad to meet these bills when they fall due and to pay London its commission for the use of these facilities.

(6) The actual rates of exchange charged for drafts in foreign currency are based on the prices at which bills on that foreign country can be bought.

APPENDIX TO CHAPTER IV

Specimen Letter of Lien

30th June, 1926

Messrs. X. & Y., Ltd.,
London, E.C.2

Dear Sirs,

In consideration of your accepting our draft value £2,500 maturing 30th September/3rd October, 1926, we give you herewith a lien on the goods as per list and copy invoices attached; and we undertake to reimburse you before the due date out of the proceeds of the sales of the said goods and to hold such proceeds as and when received in trust for you.

In payment of your accepting commission we beg to hand you our cheque value £15 12s. 6d., receipt of which please acknowledge.

Yours faithfully,

CHAPTER V

EXCHANGE TRADING

THE examination of the way foreign currency balances are built up showed that rates of exchange depend on the price of bills. Before proceeding to analyse the factors which determine the price of bills, it seems to best correlate the theory of the last chapter with the practice of exchange trading as handled in the foreign departments of the banks and reported in the daily newspapers.

In the money columns in the daily papers there are, under the heading "Foreign Exchanges," a list of figures preceded by a certain amount of descriptive wording, recording the movements in rates which occurred during the previous day, such as "marks depreciated," "dollars appreciated," etc., etc. The figures formerly represented the foreign exchange rates which were current at the close of business on the previous day in the various foreign centres. They were not the rates quoted in London, but were cabled from the foreign centres opposite the various names. To-day they represent the rates obtaining in London at the close of the previous day's business. These figures are in one of two forms. Either they mean so much of a foreign currency unit to the pound, as in the case of France, Germany, or U.S.A.—4·85 opposite U.S.A. means that you can get 4·85 dollars for £1—or they are in the form of so many pence, or shillings and pence, per foreign unit, as in the case of Brazil, where the figure 8 means that you can get a milreis for 8d.; or in the case of Japan, where the figure of 2s. 4d. means that you can get one yen for that amount. All the rates are quoted in one or other of these two forms.

There follows a list of the currencies of the principal countries of the world, including Mint Pars where such exist. The Mint Par rates, it may be repeated, represented approximately the actual rates which obtained before the war : actual rates to-day are given in the next column.

Centre	Par	Actual Rate Quoted, March 23, 1926	Currency in which Rate is Quoted
New York	4·86$\frac{2}{3}$	4·86$\frac{5}{32}$—4·86$\frac{9}{32}$	Dollar and cent.
Montreal	do.	4·87$\frac{5}{8}$—4·87$\frac{7}{8}$	do.
Paris	25·22$\frac{1}{2}$	137·65—138·80	Franc & centime.
Brussels	do.	119$\frac{1}{2}$—120$\frac{3}{4}$	do.
Geneva	do.	25·24$\frac{3}{4}$—25·25$\frac{1}{4}$	do.
Rome	do.	120·85—120·90	Lira & centesimo (*plural,* Lire & centesimi).
Athens	do.	362—363	Drachma & lepta.
Madrid	do.	34·49—34·51	Peseta & centimo.
Sofia	do.	650—670	Levz & stötinki.
Bucharest	do.	1160—1170	Lei.
Berlin	20·43	20·41—20·42	Reichsmark and pfennig.
Amsterdam	12·107	12·13$\frac{1}{4}$—12·13$\frac{1}{2}$	Florin (or Guilder) and cent.
Vienna	34·58$\frac{1}{2}$	34·48—34·52	Schilling.
Prague	24·02	164—164$\frac{1}{8}$	Krone (*plural,* Kronen).
Budapest	27·82	27·60—27·90	Pengo.
Warsaw	25·22$\frac{1}{2}$	37$\frac{1}{2}$ sellers	Zloty & grosz.
Stockholm	18·159	18·11$\frac{3}{4}$—18·12$\frac{1}{2}$	Krona & öre (*plural,* Kroner)
Oslo	do.	22·52—22·68	Krone & öre (*plural,* Kroner)
Copenhagen	do.	18·52—18·55	do.
Helsingfors	193·23	192$\frac{7}{8}$—193$\frac{1}{8}$	
Latvia	25·22$\frac{1}{2}$	25·20—25·35	Lat.
Lithuania	48·66	49·00—49·50	Lita.
Esthonia	—	1800—1840	Mark.
Batavia	12·107	12$\frac{1}{2}$	Florins.

Of the countries above, France, Belgium, Switzerland, Italy, and Greece are known as the "Latin Monetary Union."

The pre-war currency of Germany was the mark. This having lost value by the over-issue of paper money as described later, a new currency unit was issued called the Reichsmark with the same Mint Par as that of the mark.

In the case of both Austria and Hungary the pre-war currency was the krone and heller (*plural*, kronen and heller). The Mint Par of the krone was 24·02. The relation between the Austrian schilling of to-day and the krone is: 1 gold krone = 1.44 schillings; that between the krone and the pengo is 1 gold krone = 1.158 pengoes.

The currency of Poland from 1918–1924 consisted of the Polish paper mark. Taken over from the German régime, this paper currency never had a Mint Par, since its issue was not based on any Mint Laws of the Polish State. Its value in 1924 in terms of the new currency then issued was, 1,800,000 paper marks = 1 zloty.

The Esthonian mark is the currency taken over from the German occupation authorities during the war Like the Polish paper mark, and for the same reason, it has no Mint Par. The Dutch colony of Batavia has the same currency as Holland, and therefore the same par, but the rate is a different one because Batavia has its own balance of payments distinct from that of Holland.[1]

So far, it will be observed, we have quoted in every case so many units of the foreign currency to one pound. In other cases the style of quoting is different, as shown in first table on page 46.

The pre-war currency of Russia was the rouble, which lost value, like the German mark and the Austrian and Hungarian kronen, through over-issue of paper money. 1 Chervonetz = 10 gold roubles.

In the case of Brazil the milreis = 1,000 reis (Rs.) 1,000 milreis (= 1,000,000 paper reis), are called a "Conto," and large figures are generally quoted as so many "Contos of reis."

[1] See Chapter VIII.

Centre	Par	Actual Rates Quoted, March 23, 1926	Currency in which Rate is Quoted
Moscow - -	9·458	$9{\cdot}43\frac{1}{2}$	Chervonetz to £10 (*plural*, Chervonetzi).
Lisbon - -	$4{\cdot}50\frac{1}{2}$	$2{\cdot}\frac{33}{64}$–$2{\cdot}\frac{35}{64}$	Pence per escudo
Rio de Janeiro	27	$7{\cdot}\frac{3}{32}$–$7{\cdot}\frac{5}{32}$	Pence per milreis.
Valparaiso -	40	39·50	Pesos to £1.
Buenos Aires -	47·58	$43{\cdot}\frac{11}{16}$–$43{\cdot}\frac{15}{16}$	Pence per gold peso.
Monte Video -	50·98	$49\frac{3}{4}$–$50\frac{1}{4}$	do.
Lima - -	Par	$26\frac{1}{2}$% Premium	English £1 to Peruvian £1.
Kobe - -	24·5	1/10·–$1/10\frac{7}{16}$%	Shillings & pence per yen.

In the Argentine there is a double currency—the gold peso and the paper peso, of which only the latter is in actual circulation; but dealings with foreign countries are almost always conducted in terms of gold pesos or foreign currency. The currency of Paraguay consists of the paper peso, but transactions with foreign countries are generally conducted in the currency of those countries or in the Argentine gold peso.

The following are the chief silver-using centres:

Centre	Rates Quoted, March 23, 1926	Currency in which Rate is Quoted
Mexico - -	23·80–24·30	Pence per dollar.
Alexandria -	$97\frac{1}{2}$d.	Piastres to £1.
Constantinople	945–960	Do.
Shanghai -	2s. $10\frac{7}{8}$d.	Shillings and pence to 1 tael.
Hongkong -	2s. $3\frac{1}{2}$d.	Do. 1 dollar.
Singapore -	2s. $4{\cdot}\frac{3}{32}$d.	Do. 1 do.
Bangkok -	1s. $10\frac{1}{8}$d.	Do. 1 do.

India is a special case of a silver currency based on gold which will be examined in detail later. The currency unit is the rupee, a silver coin, which is divided into annas and into pieces: 1 rupee = 16 annas = 64 pieces. A lac is 100,000 rupees; a crore is 100 lacs.

Centre	Par	Actual Rate Quoted on Mar. 23, 1926	Currency in which Rate is Quoted
Calcutta -	$\frac{1}{10}$th of £1 (gold)	1s. 6d.	Shillings and pence to 1 rupee.

The following Central and South American rates are added for the purpose of completeness:

Country	Mint Par	Actual Rate ruling on Dates indicated	Currency in which Rates are Quoted
		1926	
Ecuador (Guyaquil)	10·15	Mar. 4th, 22·35	Sucres to £1
Venezuela (Caracas)	25·22	Mar. 3rd, 25·07	Bolivares to £1
Colombia: Bogota	100,000	Mar. 2nd, 98·88	Pesos to £1
Nicaragua	4·87	Mar. 6th, 4·80	Cordobas to £1
San Salvador	9·73	Mar. 6th, 9·97	Colones to £1
Guatemala	90·23	Mar. 6th, 292·00	Pesos to £1
Costa Rica	10·45	Feb. 27th, 18·92	Colones to £1
Bolivia (La Paz)	19·20	Feb. 21st, $17\frac{5}{8}$	Pence to Bolivano

In the case of Lisbon, Alexandria, the Far Eastern, and the South American centres, it is customary in the newspapers to quote also the rates obtaining in those centres on London.

The currencies of Australia and South Africa consist of Australian and South African pounds, which each contain the same weight of gold as the English pound. The Pars of exchange would take the form :

£100 (Australian) = £100 (English)
£100 (South African) = £100 (English)

Although these two currencies represent the same weight of gold as the English pound, yet the actual rates at which pounds in England are exchanged for pounds in Australia and South Africa vary just like other rates, for they are subject to the same kind of influences.[1] In the case of Australia the rate of exchange is quoted in terms of so many English pounds per Australian £100 ; thus if the Australian rate be £98½, this means that if you pay to bank in London £98 10s. they will put £100 to your credit in Sydney. In the case of South Africa the rate is quoted at so much per cent. premium or discount : thus if South African currency be at a discount of 1½ per cent. you will receive, in return for paying £98 10s. in London, £100 in Johannesburg.

The difficulty in reading exchange rates is that the prices of currencies are not quoted in the same way as other prices. The raising of the figure which indicates the price of any article is favourable from the seller's point of view, as, for example, is the case in the stock market, of which one is most likely to think when considering exchange matters. A rise in the price of shares is obviously favourable to the holders ; but a rise in the rate quoted for sterling may or may not be favourable to the holder. In the case of the dollar, clearly a higher figure does mean a more favourable rate, as it is better for us to get 4·85 dollars for our pound than 4·40 dollars. In the case of Brazil the opposite is true : in selling sterling for milreis, it is more advantageous to the seller of sterling to obtain one milreis for every 8d. than for every 10d. In

[1] See Chapter VIII.

this case the raising of the rate is unfavourable. The rule is that where the exchange is quoted in terms of foreign currency to the pound the high rate is favourable to sterling; where it is quoted in terms of pence per foreign unit, a low rate is favourable to sterling. We have been using the terms "favourable" and "unfavourable" in the sense in which the newspapers frequently use them, i.e. from the point of view of the holder of sterling, i.e. of the potential buyer of foreign currency. It is necessary to bear in mind that when the newspapers say "the French rate went further in our favour," they are speaking from the point of view of the holder of sterling who wishes to buy francs. To the holder of the currency whose rate is in question, e.g. to the English holder of German marks, the significance of the terms "favourable" and "unfavourable" will be exactly the opposite. The lower the rate, i.e. the less marks he has to give up to secure one pound, the better he will be pleased.

Now, looking at the matter from the foreigners' point of view, it will be evident that where the quotation is in terms of foreign currency to the pound, as in the case of francs, marks, and dollars, a rise in the rate means a decline in the value of those currencies, because more francs have to be surrendered to secure a pound. Similarly, a fall in the rate for francs means a rise in their value. It is this point of view which the newspaper writer is taking when, on the rate for francs declining from 130 to 120 to the pound, he says, "francs appreciated slightly": it is the value which has appreciated.

The next point in regard to the quotations in the daily papers is that they are double-barrelled—there are two quotations. These two quotations represent buyers and sellers. Suppose, for example, that on any given day 1920 the quotation opposite New York was 3·96–3·97. That means if you are buying dollars you will get 3·96 dollars for every pound you expend; if, on the other hand, you have dollars to sell, you will get £1 for every 3·97. If you went to the foreign exchange department of a bank at the time these quotations obtained, they would tell you that dollars were 3·96 buyers and 3·97 sellers, or they might have said 3·96½ middle rate. The difference between the two represents the margin for dealing. That does not mean the margin on which a private individual could encroach if he went into a bank to sell or buy dollars—he could not sell better than 3·97 or buy better than 3·96. It means the margin between the banks themselves and the foreign exchange dealers in London.

The quotation (p. 44) for the Polish zloty, " 37½ sellers " means that at the time when this rate was reported no one wanted to buy Polish currency, while those dealers who had it to sell were holding out for a rate of 37½.

We will look into these double-barrelled quotations more closely, and consider the position of four parties in this matter. The four parties are : The foreign department of a London bank; the foreign department of its Manchester branch; the outside individual in Manchester, "A," who wants to buy or sell a dollar draft; and the foreign exchange broker in London. Assume that the foreign department in London is quoting to ordinary buyers 3·96, and to ordinary sellers 3·97. It will improve on these rates to its Manchester branch, and will probably quote them 3·96¼ and 3·96¾. Thus the Manchester branch will be able to buy at better rates from its London house than " A " could if he went to London direct. Head office is able to make a better rate for Manchester because London itself, being right in the heart of the foreign exchange market, is able to buy from the foreign exchange broker at a still better rate. They will be doing business with the foreign exchange broker which will be something like 3·96⅜ and 3·96⅝. So far as London is concerned the rates are moving inwards. As a matter of fact, some brokers in London buy from a London head office and sell to them at the same rate, simply working on commission and specializing in certain currencies, just as some merchants and manufacturers' agents work entirely on a commission basis. Thus the Manchester branch has the margins between 96 and $96\frac{1}{4}$ (buying) and between $96\frac{3}{4}$ and 97 (selling); the London head office has the margins between $96\frac{1}{4}$ and $96\frac{3}{8}$ and between $96\frac{3}{4}$ and $96\frac{5}{8}$; the broker, if he is not working on commission, has the margin between $96\frac{3}{8}$ and $96\frac{5}{8}$. This example is taken from the dollar exchange, which even before the return of the pound to parity was one of the steadiest, and where the margins were consequently small and the risks few or none. In the case of the exchanges with wider fluctuations the margins are very much greater.

The broker, after a sale of currency to the bank, sends to the purchasing bank a contract note stating particulars of the currency sold and the name of the seller; this enables the bank to instruct the seller where to pay the currency. The currency is not in the form of foreign notes, but of a draft on a foreign bank; and it is paid, not to the bank itself but by its instructions to its foreign currency account in the foreign town in question. Banks keep such accounts in the principal centres abroad. They are known as "Nostro" accounts (*Latin* = our). It is on these accounts that the foreign drafts issued by banks to their customers who have bought foreign currency are issued, and from them that mail and telegraphic transfers [1] are made. Proceeds of bills and coupons sent for collection similarly go to swell the Nostro account. In the case of sale of currency by the bank to the broker, a similar contract note is passed by the broker to his purchasers, from whom the selling bank receives instructions where to pay the currency. Payment is made, of course, out of a Nostro account.

[1] See p. 7.

The actual work of buying and selling currencies in a bank is performed by the exchange trader, who is usually "second man" in the foreign department, i.e. second-in-command to the manager of the foreign department. The most go-ahead of the provincial branches of the joint-stock banks have now direct telephonic communication with their London head office, by means of which they are advised of the fluctuations in rates from minute to minute. The exchange trader's aim all the time is to balance his sales and his purchases, so that he is left neither with foreign currency on his hands nor with a liability in respect of currency which he has sold but not yet bought in. His aim, in other words, is not to make big profits by gambling on the prospects of rises or falls in exchange rates, but to accumulate margins and take as little risk as possible. He will, therefore, in so far as his sales are not covered by his purchases, cover by buying immediately from his own head office, and in so far as his purchases are not disposed of by his sales, sell immediately to his own head office. The head office trader in turn will sell to the exchange dealers; and it is the higgling of the market between head office traders and exchange dealers, who in turn have connexions abroad, which ultimately makes the final rates.

The next point to refer to in regard to the rates quoted in the daily papers is the class of draft quoted for. Different centres quote for different classes of draft. The principal kinds of drafts quoted for are:

Cable or Telegraphic transfers (T.T.) -	8-day drafts.
Sight drafts - - - - - - -	90-day drafts.

A cable transfer is the means used by a man in New York who wants to pay a man in London at once. He goes into the offices of a New York bank, instructs them to cable a certain amount of money to someone in London, and pays them a certain quantity of dollars. The bank immediately cables its London correspondents, and the latter firm pay immediately they receive the cable. That is the meaning of a cable transfer. The cable rate is the rate at which the dollars paid by the man in New York are exchanged for the sterling which the payee in London receives.

A sight draft is a draft payable at sight and goes by mail. "A" has to pay a creditor in Paris. "A" sends him a draft in francs on some French bank, payable at sight. The sight draft is the rate at which "A" buys that draft in francs from a London bank: it represents the rate at which sterling is converted into francs payable at sight in Paris.

Eight- and ninety-day drafts mean drafts payable 11 (8 plus 3 days of grace) and 93 days respectively after sight. The classes of drafts quoted in the newspapers for each of the principal centres are:

European centres -	Sight drafts.
New York - -	Cable transfer, sight, 60-day drafts.
Mexico - - -	Telegraphic transfer.
Argentine - -	,, ,,
Uruguay - - -	,, ,,
Chili - - -	90-day drafts.
Peru - - -	,, ,,
Brazil - - -	,, ,,
Bolivia - - -	60-day drafts.
Egypt - - -	Sight drafts.
Oriental centres -	Telegraphic transfers.

The sight rate is known as "Short Exchange," and the three months' rate as "Long Exchange." The three months' rate can be calculated from the short rate, and vice versa.[1] The point to remember in making these calculations is that when we buy a sight draft we are paying a dealer pounds down for francs at sight; for practical pur-

[1] For details of the calculations involved, see Spalding: "Foreign Exchange and Foreign Bills," p. 48.

poses we are paying pounds now and getting in exchange francs now. When, on the other hand, we buy a three months' draft, we are paying pounds now, and getting francs which will not materialize until three months hence. It will be evident that, in consideration of waiting, we must in the second case receive more francs for the same number of pounds than in the first: the long rate, in other words, will be higher in this case than the short rate. If we are dealing not with the currency which is quoted in terms of foreign units to the pound, but with one which is quoted in terms of so many pence to the foreign unit, with the milreis, for example, the long rate will be lower than the short: for the buyer has to be benefited in consideration of waiting, and the only way to benefit him is to reduce the number of pence he pays for each milreis.

Particular rates can be made for bills which have periods of between one and three months to run, e.g. 73 days. Such rates are known as Tel Quel (= such as it is) rates. They can be calculated from either the sight rate or the three months' rate on the principle indicated in the foregoing paragraph. They will be more favourable to the buyer of the bill than the sight rate (i.e. more francs to the pound or fewer pence to the milreis), for the buyer has to wait for his claim to the foreign currency to mature; less favourable to him than the three months' rate, for he has not to wait so long.

With one exception, bills for periods longer than three months are not common in exchange markets. A merchant who desires to discount a longer-dated bill with his bank, invites reflections as to the financial soundness of the customers with whom he is doing business: why do they require such long credit? Bills of longer than three months' maturity are drawn, but generally their use is to be held as security for a debt rather than to serve as currency. The exception occurs in the South American trade, where bills at 120 days are customary and recognized.

There is one caution it is necessary to bear in mind. In the news columns of the papers—not in the money columns—one frequently sees phrases of the type: "Yesterday the £1 was worth 18s. in New York, 41s. 6d. in Paris," and so on. That is the wrong way to think about the exchanges. A pound cannot be worth 18s. 6d. in New York, for the simple reason that in New York they do not deal in pounds, shillings, and pence. It can only be worth a certain amount of dollars. If on the day we read that the pound was worth 18s. 6d. in New York we had turned to the back page and read the money column, we should have seen that the pound was worth 4·38 dollars. What was meant was of course that a pound to-day would produce the amount of dollars, which, had the pound been at par value, could have been purchased for 18s. 6d. In other words, at pre-war values the amount of dollars which to-day will purchase £1 would only have purchased 18s. 6d. The statement that the pound was worth 18s. 6d. is a half-truth stated in a form which is sheer nonsense.

This is more than a question of words. Of the errors into which this way of thinking about the exchanges can lead, a good example is the following incident. It is given in full as it is a good exercise in exchange thinking. The subjoined letter appeared in the "Manchester Guardian" of February 27, 1920:

"I purchased an article some months ago for £600 calculated on $4·75 to the pound sterling, and agreed to pay the difference in the exchange when the goods were delivered. When I paid the cheque the pound was worth $3·25, and the papers of that day boomed the fact that the pound had touched 13s. 3d. One would think, therefore, that I should have to pay 600 times 6s. 9d., equal to £207 10s. But I am told that the difference is £277 10s., or 9s. 3d. for each pound sterling that I have already paid. If that is correct, the pound on the rate of exchange was worth only 10s. 9d. It may be simple to some people, but can anyone make it clear to me ? "

Inquiry among the author's classes in Manchester found very few who were able to point out all the fallacies in the above letter. Apart from a small mistake in arithmetic and the ignoring of the fact that his remittance was made at a rate fractionally different from the 3·25 quoted, the writer of the letter may be interested to learn, if he buys this book, that there were three fallacies in his argument.

The first and most fundamental was that the pound was never worth so many shillings and pence in the United States, but so many dollars and cents. His liability was reckoned, and could only be reckoned, in dollars and cents. This is true whether the price was quoted to him in pounds or dollars. If the price was quoted in dollars, the following calculation obtains :

Price in dollars (600 × 4·75) - - - -	= $2850
His £600 realized dollars (600 × 3·25) - -	= $1950
Difference which he had to pay - - -	$900

These 900 had to be purchased at 3·25, so that the sterling he had to expend was £(900 ÷ 3·25) = 276·923, or £276 18s. 6d.

If, on the other hand, the price was quoted to him in sterling, he had to make up the difference in exchange of $(4·75 — 3·25) = $1·5 on every pound, so that he would have to find 600 times $1·5 = $900, and to purchase that 900 dollars at 3·25. This entails an expenditure of £276 18s. 6d. as per the previous calculation. The difference between the £276 18s. 6d. at which we arrive and the £277 10s. which he actually had to pay will evidently be accounted for by the fact that at the hour when he paid his cheque, the rate was slightly below 3·25 ; 3·25 quoted by the newspapers was the closing rate for the day.

Secondly, his reasoning is wrong even if we take his own erroneous standpoint and use his own misleading terms. First of all there is an arithmetical mistake. When the pound was equivalent to \$3·25, it was "worth," in terms of pre-war pounds, $\frac{3 \cdot 25}{4 \cdot 87}$ of 20s. = 13s. 4d., so that the difference to be made up, according to his premises, would not be 6s. 9d. but 6s. 8d. multiplied by 600. But, apart from this arithmetical mistake, his reasoning is wrong even if we start from his own premises. For on the day of purchase the pound was not "worth" 20s.; it was "worth" only $\frac{4 \cdot 75}{4 \cdot 87}$ of 20s. = 19s. 6d.

The amount to be made up would therefore be not 20s. — 13s. 4d., but 19s. 6d. — 13s. 4d. = 6s. 2d.; so that on his own line of reasoning he should have paid not 600 × 6s. 8d. but 600 × 6s. 2d.

Thirdly, in calculating his liability in shillings and pence, he is throughout calculating in pre-war shillings and pence, whereas the only shillings and pence available to him in which to settle his liability were depreciated coins; the shillings and pence not of pre-war days, nor even of the day of purchase of the goods, but of the day of payment. Paying, as he has to do, in depreciated shillings and pence, he has to pay not only 6s. 2d. per pound, but something additional to make the six-and-twopences which he pays equivalent to the pre-war six-and-twopences in terms of which he has been reckoning.

Had the writer of the letter kept his mind clear of the second and third fallacies, he could, working by his own roundabout methods, have reached the correct result which is properly obtained by our first calculation above. What it was essential to remember, and what he forgot, was that when he thought "the pound is worth so many shillings and pence," what he really meant was "to-day's pound is worth so many pre-war shillings and pence";

and he should have added, "I have got to provide the equivalent in to-day's shillings of so many pre-war shillings." His calculation would have been as follows :

Number of pounds on which deficiency has to be made up - - - - - -	600
Deficiency per pound on day of payment as compared with day of purchase - - -	6s. 2d.
Each 6s. 2d. of to-day must, in order to be made equal to the pre-war 6s. 2d., be increased in ratio of - - - - - - -	$\frac{4{\cdot}867}{3{\cdot}25}$

The liability is therefore

$$\frac{6s.\ 2d. \times 600 \times 4{\cdot}867 \text{ shillings,}}{3{\cdot}25}$$

or $\frac{£{\cdot}3082 \times 600 \times 4{\cdot}867}{3{\cdot}25} = £276{\cdot}924 = £276\ 18s.\ 6d.$

All his trouble would have been avoided had he remembered that in the United States his pounds were worth so many dollars and cents. Had he remembered that, he would not have presented us with a very interesting example of the wrong way to think about exchange matters.

If we are going to think clearly on the subject of the exchanges, we must avoid half-truths such as that indicated by the statement criticized. We must think of the pound as being worth so much of the currency of the country in question.

An operation which demands a word of explanation is that of buying and selling exchange forward. Merchants do not as a rule wish to gamble in exchange, and a merchant doing business to-day with one of the numerous countries whose currency is subject to frequent fluctuations generally avoids risk by the above-named operation. If he is due to receive or to have to pay a certain quantity of foreign currency at a future date, or within a given period, he sells this currency or buys, as the case may be in advance. If he is an exporter due to receive payment in currency, he agrees to deliver to the bank on a certain day, or within a certain period, that quantity of that currency. Conversely if he is an importer due to pay a certain quantity of currency, he agrees to buy that quantity on a certain day or within a certain period. The transaction in each case is made at a rate fixed at the time. The merchant limits his liability to a definite quantity of sterling; the bank has means not available to the merchant lessening the liability of which it has relieved him. Where the bank is the forward seller, and the amount is small, it may purchase spot currency and hold it until such time as the customer requires it. Where the amount is larger, the bank in turn may buy forward. In any case, it can, if it desires, rely on its balances abroad for delivery. A forward sale, again, may be set off against a long-dated bill on the foreign centre in question, maturing on or a little before the date of delivery of the currency. Or such a long-dated bill maturing later than the said date might be discounted on or before the date of delivery. Similarly when currency is bought forward from a client, the purchase can be covered by a forward sale. Or, if, e.g. delivery of the currency is to be made by the seller to the bank in two months' time, the bank can now sell two months' drafts on the foreign centre in question.

The rates for forward purchases and sales of course vary from those for spot transactions. They may be more or less favourable to the buyer, according to the opinion held by the foreign exchange market of the likelihood that during the near future the currency in question will appreciate or depreciate. Thus, e.g. on February 19, 1926, the "Manchester Guardian" quoted the rates on certain centres for settlement one month forward as follows. The rates for two and three months forward are usually approximately twice or thrice those quoted for one month forward.

New York - -	$\frac{1}{4}$ to $\frac{3}{16}$ cent. under spot.
Brussels - -	13 to 18 centimes under spot.
Paris - - -	- 20 to 25 centimes over spot.
Italy -	27 to 32 centesimi under to one over spot.
Holland - - -	$2\frac{1}{2}$ to 2 cents under spot.
Bombay (3 months' tel. transfers) -	$\frac{1}{32}$d. under spot.

The above means that the market thought on February 18, 1926, that the Belgian franc would improve during the coming month and that the Dutch and Indian rate would also do so very slightly; hence it would then be necessary to give up less of those currencies in exchange for one pound than on February 18th. The Italian and the New York rates were conceived as steady; hence the forward rate was practically the same as the spot rate. The French franc, on the other hand, was considered likely to depreciate in value during the coming month; hence it would then be necessary to surrender more francs in exchange for one pound than was necessary on February 18th.

CHAPTER VI

DOCUMENTARY BILLS AND CREDITS

IT has been explained in outline how foreign bills feed the foreign currency balances of the banks, and how the exchange trader operates on those balances at rates which are fixed by the factors ruling in the foreign exchange market. Before we proceed to analyse these factors,[1] it is best to complete our mental picture of the foreign exchange world by examining in detail some of the more important credit operations between bankers and merchants centring round the foreign bill. This chapter is accordingly devoted to the detailed procedure for dealing with foreign bills.

The first distinction to make is that between clean and documentary bills. A documentary bill is a bill which has attached to it the shipping documents covering the goods in respect of which the bill is drawn. A clean bill is a bill without such documents attached. The documents in question are:

(*a*) Invoice.
(*b*) Bill of lading.
(*c*) Consular invoice.
(*d*) Insurance policy or insurance certificate.
(*e*) Letter of hypothecation, particular or general.

Invoice, bill of lading, and consular invoice are straightforward enough, but we must say a word about the letter of hypothecation and the insurance policy. A letter or certificate of hypothecation is an instrument in and by virtue of which the drawer of the draft makes legal acknowledgments which constitute any holder of the draft also the holder of the bill of lading and insurance certificate as collateral security. What that means is this: the bank

[1] See Chapter VIII.

has the draft, it has the documents covering the goods, and it requires a further document to show that it has a legal right to the document covering the goods. A hypothecation certificate is that document. It gives a banker a good title to the documents which cover the goods. A hypothecation certificate may be particular or general. Where the transaction is an isolated one, the bank will have a form of letter of hypothecation applicable to that kind of draft, probably a printed form which the drawer of the draft will sign and send along with the bill and documents. Where, however, the business is a regular, steady, and sound one, conducted by exporters well known to the bank, and the foreign importers also well known to the bank, then it is quite likely that the bank will be satisfied with a general letter of hypothecation, by which the drawer of the draft hypothecates to the bank all the documents attached to all his drafts which the bank discounts for him. In such a case, again, the bank will not require an insurance policy itself, but will accept in lieu thereof an insurance certificate, i.e. a certificate from a firm of insurance brokers to the effect that the goods in question have been insured. Insurance policies attached to bills are forwarded by the bank to whom the documentary draft is entrusted for collection to its collecting branch, if claims under such policies are payable abroad; if claims are payable in the country of the drawer, the policies are retained by the first-named bank unless it is specially requested to forward them to its collecting branch.

The next point in connexion with documentary drafts is the distinction between D/A and D/P drafts. A D/A draft means that the documents attached to the draft are to be surrendered on acceptance of the draft; a D/P draft means that the documents are not to be surrendered until the draft is paid. The custom is for the drawers of the bill, when sending it to their bank for negotiation, or for collection and remittance of the proceeds as the case may be, to cover it with a letter in which they say that the documents attached to the draft are to be surrendered only on acceptance, or only on payment of the draft. Or, alternatively, in place of such a letter, they attach a slip to the draft embodying the same statement. Where nothing is stated it is always understood that a documentary draft is a D/P draft. From the point of view of the bank making the advances against the documentary draft, clearly the D/P bill is the safer. It is conceivable that the drawees might accept a D/A draft, get the documents, and then dishonour the bill. In the case of a D/P draft, they cannot get the documents until they have paid the bill. However, as we shall see, both kinds of drafts are suitable on occasion for the bank to advance money against, while on occasion neither may be suitable. It all depends upon the circumstances of each particular case. There are some markets, South American chiefly, where business is nearly always done with D/A drafts, and in other markets it frequently happens that where the drawers are starting business with the drawees they will use D/P drafts for the first two or three shipments, and D/A drafts afterwards.

We now come to the question of banks' advances against drafts. A documentary draft may be negotiated either before or after acceptance. Here we need only repeat in outline the case taken earlier, when we saw how foreign bills served as currency.[1] We took the case where a British firm was shipping goods to Sweden and drawing on the Swedish consignees, whom we called Franssons. The drawers would draw, let us say, a sixty days' sight draft D/A on Franssons; and the draft might be dealt with in one of various ways.

(*a*) If the drawers have an agent in Stockholm, they would send the documentary draft to that agent, the

[1] See Chapter IV.

agent would present the draft to Franssons, get it accepted by them, and hand over to Franssons the documents. Franssons could then get the goods while the agent might return the draft to the British exporter, who would then sell it either to his bank or to a London bill-broker, from either of whom the draft would find its way on to the London foreign exchange market.

(*b*) If the British exporter had no agent in Stockholm, but nevertheless did a good business in Sweden, which necessitated paying out as well as paying in in Sweden, he might very well keep a foreign currency account at a bank in Sweden, let us say the Skandinaviska Kreditaktiebolaget in Stockholm. In that case, he would send the draft to that bank, they would present it to Franssons, get it accepted and hand over the documents ; and having now the draft in the form of a clean bill, the bank might either hold it until the draft matured, then present it for payment and credit the British exporter's account at that date, or it might discount the bill at once and credit the British exporter's account at once.

(*c*) Again, in place of the agent returning the draft to the British exporter, he himself might have sold it to his Swedish bank, say the Nordiska Handelsbanken, in Stockholm. In return he would receive this bank's draft in kroner, drawn on another Stockholm bank, which he would send to the British exporter to be sold on the London Foreign Exchange market.

These are the outlines of the various procedures which might be followed. They all have this in common : that the draft is not discounted until it has been accepted. In that sense the foreign bill on Franssons is just like an ordinary home trade bill of exchange.

Now suppose that instead of being a D/A draft it had been a D/P draft. In that case Franssons would not have been able to get the goods until they had not only accepted, but also paid the draft. It may be asked,

What good was the draft to them ? They would be able to inspect the goods, and during the 60 days sell them, so that immediately they got the documents they could hand them straight over to the ultimate buyers. There is another possibility in regard to a D/P draft : Franssons might like to pay under a rebate ; in other words, they might not wait until the 60 days were up, but pay the draft before, and obtain a rebate of the proportionate amount of interest. It is of course possible that after Franssons had originally accepted the D/P draft and given it back to the bank, the bank might have detached the draft from the documents, and sold it clean. In that case Franssons could still have paid the draft under rebate of a proportionate amount of the interest, and the bank would have given them the documents, together with a guarantee that when the holder of the draft presented it for payment the bank itself would pay. Even a D/P draft can in that way become a clean bill.

All these cases are relatively simple. They all have the characteristic that there is no question of discounting until the draft is accepted. Now we come to a more complicated case, in which the money is advanced against the draft before it is accepted. It is quite evident that there must be some kind of arrangement whereby that can be done, because the procedure we have outlined, while useful for Sweden and the nearer continental countries, would not be of very much use in regard to Eastern and South American markets, and we find accordingly that there are ways whereby the banks can and do advance money against drafts before acceptance. To such an extent in fact is that the case, that there are markets and trades in which it is customary for the bank to advance money not only against D/P bills before acceptance, but also against D/A drafts before acceptance, and sometimes even without the original documents accompanying the drafts. It is customary, for instance, in certain lines of business in Brazil for the original bill of lading to be sent direct to the Brazilian importer by the British exporter, and the documentary draft has attached to it, in place of the original bill of lading, only a duplicate. That means that the importer in Brazil can get possession of the goods without even accepting the draft. Nevertheless, it is customary for one of the first-class foreign banks in London to advance to British exporters of the first class the face value of such D/A drafts. The whole fact of the matter is this: in dealing with the question of banks' advances against documentary drafts, it is simply a question of deciding each case on its own merits. Inquiries have to be made regarding the customs of the particular trade in question, the class of business being done, and the financial standing and repute of the drawer and drawee. When a bank has made an advance against a documentary draft before acceptance, the procedure is for it to advise the drawer when the draft has been accepted, and again when it has been paid, at the same time sending him a statement relating to the bill. The statement will run in some such form as this:

"We beg to advise you that your remittance No. 4672/5183 [firm's number of draft and bank's own number] has been paid. As we advanced you the face value of this draft, we shall be obliged if you will refund us the amount undernoted."

	£	s.	d.
Commission, @ ⅛ per cent. - -		6	4
Foreign Bill Stamps - - - -		5	4
Postage - - - - - - -		1	0
Cables - - - - - - -		2	6
——Days' Interest, @ —— per cent. -	1	19	3
	£2	14	5

Such a statement is sent where the bank advanced the

face value of the draft. Frequently, however, the bank advances a proportion of the face value, say 80 per cent., paying to the drawer the balance, less charges, only when advice of payment is received. The bank's statement to the drawer then reads as follows:

By Proceeds of your Draft No.						£118	11	1
Less—Commission, @ —— per cent.		s.	d.					
		6	4					
Foreign Bill Stamps		5	4					
Postage		1	0					
							12	8
						117	18	5
	£	s.	d.					
To amount advances against above bill	95	0	0					
Interest —— days, @ —— per cent.	1	19	3					
						96	19	3
Balance in cheque herewith						£20	19	2

The rates of interest charged on advances against bills vary in accordance with the movement of rates generally in the money market.[1]

The inquiries which a bank will make when asked to advance money against a documentary bill vary with each particular case. If, for example, a bank is approached by, let us say, an English export firm of small proportions and little standing, the bank will probably want to know a good deal about the business to which the draft relates. The firm asking for the advance may be asked to produce the order from the foreign importer and the invoice from

[1] See Chapter XI.

the English manufacturer from whom it obtained the goods. The bank will also want to know whether the foreign importer is a firm of good standing, not likely to refuse to take up the goods, and if the English manufacturer is also a firm of good standing, whose goods can be relied upon. If all these conditions are fulfilled, then the bank will probably make an advance of perhaps 80 per cent. of the value. If these conditions are not complied with, they will not.

Another case of a bill being negotiated before acceptance occurs where an accepting house has agreed to accept bills drawn upon itself up to a certain amount. If, for example, a Brazilian exporter of coffee could go to his bank and produce a letter from one of the big merchant bankers in London, agreeing to accept bills drawn on themselves at so many days date, up to a certain amount, accompanied by shipping documents covering a certain shipment, in that case the bank at Rio de Janeiro would have no hesitation in making an advance to the face value of the bill, simply because it knows the status of the London accepting house.

The next subject to be dealt with in connexion with documentary drafts is that of documentary credits. Documentary credits serve as a means of financing foreign business in cases where otherwise the possibility of negotiating drafts before acceptance would not exist. In the case of a documentary credit, there are four parties to take into consideration: the buyer, the buyer's bank, the seller, and a bank in the seller's country. Assume the buyer to be a London merchant, the seller a New York exporter. The buyer's London bank is "A" and the seller's bank in New York is "B." The terms of sale of the goods require the opening of a credit with "B" available against shipping documents. The procedure in very broad outline is this: the buyer instructs "A" to open a credit with "B" in favour of the sellers to cover the shipment of the goods in question. " A " communicates with " B " by mail or telegram, and " B " notifies the sellers that a credit has been opened with " B " to finance the shipment of the goods specified in the advice. The principle is that " A," having charge of the buyer's account and being therefore in a position to debit that account, is able without risk to itself to authorize " B " to make payments ; " B " is willing to act on the authorization of another bank ; while the seller is willing to ship on learning from " B," his own bank, that " B " will make payment against the shipping documents. The actual manner in which " B " will make payment varies according to the terms of the credit as transmitted by " A " from the buyer. (1) " B " may pay cash over the counter in exchange for the shipping documents either unaccompanied by any draft, or (2) accompanied by a sight draft on " B," or (3) " B " may, in exchange for the shipping documents, accept, say, a 90 days' sight draft drawn by the seller on " B." Or again (4) " B " may negotiate a sight or date draft on the buyer. Such a draft will be in dollars, for a seller who is in a strong enough position to demand the opening of a credit before he ships the goods will certainly insist on the terms of that credit enabling him to draw in his own currency.

In all four cases " B " will debit " A's " account in its books with the amount expended as on the date of payment ; or alternatively if " A " does not keep an account with " B," the latter will obtain a refund of its payments from the local bank which keeps " A's " dollar balance in New York. " B," or the New York bank which keeps " A's " account will advise " A " by cable of the dollar amount with which " A " has been debited, and will confirm by mail.

In case (4), where the procedure has been by way of " B " negotiating a dollar draft on the buyer, " B " will mail the draft to " A " and " A " will present it to the drawee, i.e. the buyer, for payment. It will be paid by "A" debiting the buyer's account in its books with the amount of sterling required, on the day of payment, to buy a sight draft on New York for the amount of dollars specified on the draft. The draft itself will contain a clause providing that the drawee shall also pay interest for the period from the date of the draft to the date of payment at the stated rate. The debiting of the buyer's account in "A's" books with this interest amount will compensate "A" for the loss of interest in New York on the amount with which "A" was debited by "B."

In the other three cases, (1), (2), and (3), "A" will then debit the buyer's account in its books, as on the date on which payment was made in New York, with the sterling equivalent of the dollars with which it has been debited in New York. The question arises as to the rate of exchange applied. Theoretically, the rate should be that at which "A" has presumably had to replenish its dollar balance, i.e. the cable rate obtaining on the day when it received cable advice that the payment had been made. When we speak of the cable rate we mean, of course, the cable rate quoted in the London exchange market adjusted by the bank's exchange trader in the manner already described.[1] But in actual fact "A" will have the option of two rates: first the one mentioned, and second the earlier rate obtaining on the day when the buyer gave instructions for the credit to be opened. "A" will almost certainly choose the rate less favourable to sterling, i.e. the rate at which the given quantity of dollars paid out by "B" means a greater amount of sterling; and will debit the buyer with the greater amount, irrespective of the rate at which it has in fact replenished its New York balance. The margin between the rates which it has applied to the buyer and that at which it

[1] See Chapter V.

actually covered its sale of dollars to him represents a profit on exchange to the bank over and above the normal margin on the rates charged to its customers.

A point arises in regard to the words "shipping documents" specified in the advice opening the credit. The documents required are of course the invoice, bill of lading, consular invoice, hypothecation certificate, and insurance policy. But the question may be important as to whether a policy is actually required or whether an insurance certificate, which in commercial usage is more or less equivalent to an insurance policy, will do? In practice some banks will accept what is commonly known as an insurance certificate in place of an insurance policy. An insurance certificate is really an insurance broker's contract note to produce the policy. Another form of insurance certificate consists of a certificate from the shippers of the goods to the effect that the goods have been insured under a floating policy. Still another form of insurance certificate is common in the United States, consisting of a certificate signed by the holder of the floating policy and countersigned by the insurance company which issued the floating policy. Now the issue is, will any one of those documents serve in place of an insurance policy, given that the terms on which the bank is authorized to negotiate the bills require that the bills be accompanied by shipping documents including insurance policy? The actual procedure followed by banks varies. Some banks insist upon the production of the full insurance policy, and thereby succeed in creating considerable difficulty in the export trade, and in making merchants wait for their money. Other banks will accept an insurance certificate in the first sense, i.e. a broker's contract note to produce the policy. That, however, makes the bank itself liable in respect of any claim which may be made by the drawee of the draft by reason of the fact that the insurance policy has not accompanied the draft. A ruling to that effect has been laid down in a number of cases,[1] and legally it is quite certain that where an insurance policy is specified, an insurance certificate will not suffice. Nothing will suffice except the policy. However, there is an easy way out of the difficulty created by the conflict of legal rule and commercial practice: any bank will be safe in accepting a certificate where a policy is stipulated for provided that in addition to the certificate it gets also from the importer a letter of indemnity. A letter of indemnity is a letter signed by the exporter, and countersigned by the exporter's own bank advancing the money indemnified against any claims that may be made against it by reason of the fact that it has accepted the insurance certificate in place of the insurance policy.

A letter of indemnity will also be obtained by a banker who pays out of a credit which stipulates for clean bills of lading, whereas the actual bills of lading are marked "a few bags torn."

A documentary credit such as we are discussing may be either confirmed or unconfirmed. The difference between the two is that in the case of the unconfirmed credit "B" does not guarantee, as principal, that the draft drawn under the terms of the credit will be duly honoured. The implication and the difference are best illustrated by comparing the two forms of letter sent out by a well-known bank advising sellers of the opening of a confirmed and unconfirmed credit respectively. The two letters are in exactly the same form with the exception of the last sentence. In the case of the confirmed credit the last sentence reads:

"We undertake that all drafts drawn in conformity with the terms of this credit will meet with due honour on presentation, provided they are marked as being so drawn."

[1] *Livingstone* v. *Ireland* (1872) is the leading (House of Lords) case with which *Wilson Holgate* v. *Belgian Grain & Produce Co.*. (1919) and *Diamond Alkali Export Corporation, Ltd.* v. *H. Bourgeois* (1922) are in line.

In the case of the unconfirmed credit the last sentence reads:

"We have no authority from our clients to confirm this credit or to guarantee the acceptance or payment of drafts drawn there against. The credit is therefore subject to cancellation without notice, and the above particulars are for your guidance only."

From the point of view of the seller, therefore, the difference between the two forms of credit amounts practically to this: that the confirmed credit is irrevocable, whereas the unconfirmed can be revoked at any time by instructions. That difference appears clearly from two letters sent out by another bank relating to a confirmed and an unconfirmed credit:

"Confirmed Credit No. ——. Kindly note under instructions by telegram we have been requested by —— [a foreign bank] to open a confirmed credit in your favour on account of —— [the foreign client] for £—— available by your drafts on us at sight against the following documents:

"Invoice issued in the name of ——

"Bills of Lading, full set, issued to order and endorsed in blank.

"Insurance policy, marine and war, covering particular average evidencing shipment of the goods.

"Shipment to be effected on or before —— per S.S. —— from —— to ——. Drafts drawn under this credit must be presented to us on or before 28th February, 1922. All drafts must bear the number and reference mentioned above, and we undertake to honour such drafts on presentation provided they are drawn and presented in conformity with the terms of this credit."

"Unconfirmed Credit No. ——. We beg to inform you that a credit has been opened with us in your favour by order and for account of ——— [the foreign clients] to the extent of £—— available at sight against delivery of the following documents:

"Invoice.

"Bills of Lading, full set relative to shipment of goods. As we have no authority to confirm this credit to you, we are merely passing on this advice on the understanding that it is not intended to convey any engagement on the part of this bank nor any responsibility for the use you may make of this communication, as our client's instructions may be withdrawn at any time."

It is evident that from the point of view of the merchant the difference between a confirmed and an unconfirmed credit is that the former is irrevocable and the latter can be revoked. From the point of view of the banker the difference is that in the case of the confirmed credit the banker does, and in the case of the unconfirmed credit the banker does not, himself guarantee as principal to the seller that the seller's draft drawn in accordance with that credit will be met.

Unfortunately we are compelled to leave there the question of confirmed and unconfirmed credits. Beyond that point the law is vague. Most parts of the banking law are reasonably clear. Bankers are fortunate in that the banking law has been codified in the Bills of Exchange Act, but this subject of confirmed and unconfirmed credits has not been fully elucidated, and what the rights and liabilities of the various parties to credits are, in the event of one or other of them not fulfilling their obligations, has not yet been settled authoritatively in the courts. It has not yet been made certain what the position of a banker would be who paid out money under an unconfirmed credit which was revoked after he had paid the money out in ignorance of revocation.

On the general subject of credits it may be added that

the liability which the banker incurs in opening a credit is identical with the liability he incurs in making advances,[1] and a corresponding amount of care is therefore necessary. Thus in regard to shipping documents it will have been observed in one of the letters quoted that the bills of lading are to be made out to order, and endorsed in blank: this is in order that the banker can if necessary get control of the goods. There is also this further safeguard employed in some cases: where the bank "A" is asked to open a credit for its clients, it inquires of those clients as to whether they themselves have sold the goods; if they have the bank may strengthen its own position by requiring the final purchasers themselves to open a credit through their own bank. That credit will of course be at least equal in amount to, if not greater than, the amount of the credit which bank "A" has itself opened. The second credit is known as a counter-credit, and the operation relating to the opening of these two credits, the second of which balances and safeguards the first, is technically known as "marrying credits."[2] By that procedure the banker "A" who is first asked to open a credit has security afforded not only by his own client, but also by the second purchaser and the latter's bank.

Documentary credit business has increased considerably since the war. It affords a means of doing business suitable to the decline in business confidence which has been a natural result of the war. It is likely that this growth in the documentary credit business will continue: first because there are at present no signs, and no reason why there should be signs, of a restoration of business confidence to the extent to which it existed before the war; and secondly because this documentary credit business corresponds to the natural specialization of

[1] See article on "The Financing of Foreign Trade" in the "Bankers' Magazine" of December, 1919.

[2] For a full description of this procedure, see article cited in foregoing footnote.

functions. Bankers are the specialized dealers of the financial world in credit and finance, and this documentary credit business means in effect the putting of the finance and credit side of business transactions in their hands. In other words, it is the banker's business to know to what extent credit can safely be given.

A few isolated points remain to be considered in connexion with foreign bills. The first is that of bills for Collection. A bill sent for collection may of course be either D/A or D/P, either sight or date. As contrasted with the bill which is negotiated or against which an advance is made, a bill for collection is accepted for collection only, and the drawer's account is credited only when the bill is advised by the collecting bank on the other side as having been paid. This raises the question: How are foreign bills paid? The question of course relates only to bills drawn in sterling on a foreign centre. Obviously where a bill is drawn by an English firm on a Swedish one in Stockholm in kroner, then clearly it will be paid in kroner. What we have to consider is the case of a bill drawn by an English firm on a Swedish firm in sterling. The Swedish drawee can of course only pay in kroner. The question is at what rate he is to pay kroner for the sterling specified on the bill. The rule is, subject to the bill not being claused in any particular way, and subject to there not being any overriding trade custom, that the rate of exchange for a bill in sterling on a foreign centre is the rate ruling in that centre for sight drafts on London on the day of maturity of the bill. In the case named, the Swedish drawee will have to hand over to the collecting bank in Stockholm such an amount of kroner as will, on the date of maturity of the bill, purchase a sight draft on London to the face value of the bill. Supposing for example the bill is for £20, and there is no interest clause in it, and the rate for sight drafts on London on the day of maturity is 18 kr. = £1, then the amount of kroner the drawee will have to pay is $18 \times 20 = 360$ kr. The collecting bank in Stockholm will of course advise the collecting bank in London which sent it the bill for collection that the bill has been paid, and will send them a statement showing so many kroner to their credit, being the quantity of kroner paid by the drawee less collecting charges and commission. The London bank which received the bill from the drawer for collection will on receipt of that statement advise the drawer that the bill has been paid and that his account has been credited with the face value of the bill less collecting charges and commission charged by the home collecting bank. It may be of course that the drawer is in the habit of drawing a number of drafts on Sweden, and that he has payments to make in Sweden; in that case he will very likely find it to his advantage to keep a foreign currency account at a Swedish bank, and in that case he will send his bills for collection not through his own bank here, but direct to his Swedish bank, thus saving himself the commission to the English bank, which he would otherwise have to pay.

To avoid any doubt arising, a "payable" clause is generally inserted in a bill reading, "Payable at the rate for demand drafts on London." Frequently it is a little more precise: "Payable at the drawing rate for the bank's demand drafts on London." An example of such a bill is the following:

"At sixty days' sight pay this first of Exchange (second and third being unpaid) to the order of ——— Bank the sum of £—— with interest added hereto at 6 per cent. per annum from date hereof to approximate due date of arrival of remittance in London.

"Payable at the current drawing rate for the ——— Bank's draft at sight on London.

"Value received, etc., etc."

That is a slightly more precise clause than that previously

employed, and means payable at the rate at which the collecting bank's branch in the place on which the bill is drawn can draw on their London correspondents. The reason for naming the bank is simply that there may be two or three slightly different rates for demand drafts on London according to the quality of the drafts, and for that reason, in order to avoid any possibility of argument on the other side, the name of the bank is inserted. The rate at which the bank named can draw on their London correspondents will vary in accordance with the general fluctuations of exchange rates between the foreign centre in question and London.

Where the drawee pays a bill by a draft on London drawn on a bank other than the collecting bank itself—such a draft is known as a "cross draft"—the collecting bank charges the drawer a double commission, the reason being that half of the business of collection has gone through a competing bank's hands.

If in a foreign centre there is a particular custom governing the payments of drafts in sterling, then the bill will be claused in accordance with that custom. In Brazil, for example, it is the custom to pay, not by sight drafts on London, but by 90 days' sight drafts on London, and bills to Brazil are customarily claused accordingly: "Payable at the current drawing rate for 90 days' sight drafts on London." Similarly in the Argentine, where there are two currencies in existence, the gold peso and the paper peso, bills are frequently claused: "Payable in gold currency at the current drawing rate for sight drafts on London." Where there is a particular custom in the market on which the bill is drawn, it is most desirable that the bill should be claused in accordance with it, otherwise it is extremely likely there will be trouble at the other end. If for example a drawee in Brazil, when he pays sterling drafts on himself, customarily does it by handing over to the bank the number of milreis which will purchase a 90 days' sight draft on London, and on one occasion he is told to hand over the larger number of milreis that are required to purchase a sight draft on London, he will probably refuse. The chief cases where it is customary to pay by drafts other than sight drafts are those of certain South American countries, where the custom in regard to payment is as follows :

Country.	*Draft usually drawn.*	*Paid by draft on London at*
Brazil.	120 days' sight or date.	90 days' sight.
Chili.	90 days' sight	90 days' sight.

Drafts on Argentine, Uruguay, and Colombia are usually at 120 days' sight or date, those on Peru at 90 days' sight; but in these cases the customary method of payment is by sight draft on London. Again, a bill may be claused "Exchange as per Endorsement," which means that the rate of payment is to be the rate endorsed on the bill. Formerly it was the custom for the collecting bank to endorse the rate ; differences, however, occurred between the drawee and the collecting bank at the other end, and in consequence banks now prefer the seller of the bill to endorse the rate, so that in case of dispute the drawee and drawer can settle it between themselves.

Where an advance has been made by a banker against a bill which is paid by means of a 90 days' sight draft, the interest of which the banker claims the refund, or which he deducts from his advance, as the case may be, is charged for the whole period from the date of his advance to the date, not of the arrival of the 90 days' sight draft, but of the maturity of that draft.

It may happen in the case of a sterling bill drawn on Stockholm that the Swedish drawee happens to have at his disposal a certain quantity of sterling, and he may prefer to pay the bill by means of a sterling cheque for its face value rather than pay kroner. That procedure might be advantageous to him if he had bought the sterling a little time before, and by the time the bill became due kroner had gone down in value. He preferred to use his sterling rather than pay kroner. There would be no reason why the drawer of the bill should not accept the drawee's proposal, for all he desires is to get the face value of the bill, but the collecting bank must first get the assent of the drawer to the proposition. Once a bank has been handed over a bill for collection, it is not authorized to vary its terms in any way whatever, and since the bill is claused "Payable at the drawing rate for demand drafts on London," it had to be paid in that way, unless the assent of the drawer was obtained to vary those terms.

Two sources of difficulty have arisen in recent years in regard to the collection of foreign bills which did not exist before the war. The first has arisen in some continental countries by reason of the idea, widespread among modern governments, that they are superior to the laws of economics. Governments have endeavoured by law to alter the rates at which payment was made in respect of bills drawn in sterling, to the advantage of their own nationals. Such attempts have been made in Belgium and Portugal. The rule, as we have stated, is that a bill in sterling had to be paid by that amount of foreign currency which would purchase a draft at sight on London for the full face value of the bill. In Belgium a law was passed to the effect that foreign bills could be paid either in Belgium francs or in the foreign currency in question, at the option of the drawee. In Portugal an attempt was made to evade the rule by decreeing that foreign bills were to be paid at a rate fixed by the Government from time to time. Supposing for example that the market rate on any given day was 50 escudos to the pound; the Government might fix the rate at 45; clearly 45 escudos would purchase less sterling than 50; so that the Portuguese drawee paid less than he should have done, and the English drawer received less for his bill than he should have done. One is glad to say that both these attempts failed. A number of protests were made, which in the case of Belgium were effective. In the case of Portugal, shipments simply ceased until the Government was forced to rescind the decree. The second difficulty arises out of more general causes and is not avoidable.[1] Supposing a bill is received by the Swiss banking correspondent of a London bank to whom the bill has been sent by the British drawer for collection. It reaches the Swiss bank at 11 o'clock; the bank sends out for its payment immediately, having of course noted on it the quantity of Swiss francs required to purchase a sight draft on London for the face value of the bill. The drawee, who is somewhere in the country, pays that number of francs, but by the time the francs reach the Swiss collecting bank the rate has altered, and gone against Switzerland, and the number of francs will no longer purchase a sight draft on London for the face value of the bill, but will only purchase a draft for rather less than that amount. The collecting bank has done its duty by sending the bill out immediately it received it, and the drawee has paid the amount of francs for which he was asked, and which at the time he paid them would have purchased a sight draft on London. The drawer, however, gets less than the full face value of the bill, owing to the fact that between 11 o'clock and 3 o'clock there has been a fluctuation in the exchange rates, over which none of the parties concerned had any control. Had the fluctuation been in the other direction, the collecting bank would probably have pocketed the difference; but as it is, the drawer has to stand the loss.

That is more likely to happen on the Continent than here, because communications are frequently worse there, and there is in some parts a tendency to take things more

[1] See the "Bankers' Magazine" of November, 1919, on "Foreign Collections' Difficulties."

easily than we do here. Business customs being what they are, it would probably be unreasonable to expect the amount of celerity in collecting drafts which the business man expects from bankers in this country.

The next question is that of interest. Whether or not interest is added to the sum which the drawee has to pay will depend upon whether the bill does or does not contain an interest clause. If it does not, then interest will not come into the question. It may be that the drawer has added interest when making up the face value of the bill, or it may be that for business reasons he does not propose to charge interest. If interest is to be added to the face value of the bill, it must be claused accordingly. The clause will be in this form: "Pay ——— the sum of £——— with interest added hereto at ——— per cent. per annum from date hereof to the approximate due date of arrival of remittance in London." The collecting bank on the other side will calculate the approximate date of the arrival of its remittance in London, and will calculate interest for the period between the date of the bill and the date of arrival of remittance in London at the rate stated on the bill. This amount of interest will be added to the quantity of currency which the drawee has to pay to the collecting bank on the other side. At what figure the drawer originally fixes the rate will vary in accordance with (*a*) general interest rates, and (*b*) the custom of the particular centre on which the bill is drawn.

Another matter to be mentioned is that a bill may be dishonoured either by non-acceptance or by non-payment. When a bill is dishonoured, the holder must give notice of dishonour to all the parties to the bill whom he intends to hold liable on it, e.g. the drawer and previous endorsers. In the case of a foreign bill, the bill must also be noted and protested, before a notary. The holder can then, if necessary, sue any of these parties to enforce their liability. Sometimes a party is named in a bill to whom it may be presented in the event of dishonour; such party is called the "Reference in case of need" or the "Case of need." When the drawee cannot be found, or refuses to accept, or is legally debarred from accepting—e.g. an infant—another person may with the holder's consent intervene and accept; but in this case the bill must first be protested. Such an acceptance is known as "acceptance for honour" or "acceptance supra protest."

Finally, many drawers of bills seem to be unaware that they can save the payment of a double commission to the bank which collects their foreign draft by entrusting it to a bank which has a branch in the place of business of the drawee. Where such is not the case, the bank to whom the draft is handed for collection has to employ another bank to present it to the drawee, and the drawer pays the commission charged by this second bank as well as that charged by his own. Half of this commission could have been saved by sending the draft for collection to the London office of a bank specializing in the area in which the drawee's place of business is found.

CHAPTER VII

MISCELLANEOUS PRACTICAL ISSUES

IN one direction the depreciation and fluctuation of the exchanges which have been characteristic of the post-war period has led to particularly interesting and unexpected results. This is in the calculation of customs duties. It clearly makes a great difference, when duties are being calculated on the foreign currency in which the invoice is made out, whether that currency is converted at the par value or at the exchange of the day. The following quotation from the "Bulletin of the Federation of British Industries," dated September 27, 1921, which deals with the position in New Zealand, at a time when the pound was considerably below its par value as compared with the dollar, but less depreciated in value than were the franc and the lira, puts the issue very clearly:

"Take an article whose value in British currency is £100 and on which the British preferential tariff is 20 per cent., and the general tariff 30 per cent. The duty on this article, if imported from Great Britain, is at present levied by the New Zealand Customs authorities on the U.K. price, i.e. £100 plus a charge of 10 per cent. made by the Customs to cover the cost of freight, packing, and insurance. The total sum on which duty is payable is therefore £110, which at 20 per cent. equals £22 duty.

"A similar article is worth in the United States about $389 (at an average exchange rate of $3·89 = £1). It might be expected that on the 30 per cent. basis for non-British goods the duty on the American article would amount to £33. What actually happens is that the cost price of $389 is converted at the Mint Par of exchange of 4·86 = £1. This gives an equivalent in British currency of only £80, or £88 with the additional 10 per cent. duty.

Calculated on this sum the duty payable at 30 per cent. amounts to £26 8s. Instead, therefore, of the British article receiving a full 10 per cent. preference, the actual preference is only about 4 per cent.

"It is a matter for congratulation that a cable was received on September 19th by the High Commissioner for New Zealand in London, stating that as from the beginning of next year this method of assessing duty would be discarded. Instead, the New Zealand Customs authorities will assess the duty to be paid on goods imported from countries with an appreciated currency on the bank or current rate of exchange. This means that the British manufacturer will secure the full preference granted to him by the New Zealand Customs tariff."

It is evident that if the par rates are taken as the basis of calculation, countries with a depreciated rate of exchange are penalized in comparison with countries whose rates have not depreciated, or not depreciated to so great an extent. In the case of Australian duties, French, Italian, and Belgian exporters were protesting in 1919 against the use of par rates. These rates placed them at a disadvantage against British competitors for precisely the same reason that, in the case of New Zealand taken up by the F.B.I., British exporters were placed at a disadvantage with American. In the case of Australia, however, the British exporters' interest was the same as that of the American exporter in the case of New Zealand: he was competing against exports sold in depreciated currencies. In the case of Australia, therefore, the British exporter used the argument that if the duty were calculated at current rates of exchange, countries with a depreciated currency would enjoy an unfair advantage, because a pound would purchase more in those countries than in Britain. This last assumption, though probable, is by no means always true. When and how far it is true depends on the extent to which home prices have approximated to world prices; and this in turn depends on whether the depreciated currency is steady at its low level, and for how long it has been so. If a currency remains steady at some new level, home and world prices will tend to approximate, in which case the only fair way of calculating customs duties is on the basis now adopted by New Zealand, i.e. taking current rates of exchange. So long, however, as considerable fluctuations occur, hardship to somebody is inevitable, whichever method is adopted.

Another operation which requires mention is that of arbitrage. Exchange arbitrage is similar to the corresponding operation in stock and shares. The arbitrage dealer, or cambist, is an exchange dealer in country "A" who buys or sells currency of country "B" in the foreign exchange market of country "C" in order immediately to sell it again at a profit in country "A" or "B." Suppose, for example, that in the autumn of 1921 Berlin had been making heavy payments for American wheat, and the New York Exchange had moved against Berlin to the extent that in Berlin the dollar was quoted at 510 paper marks. The Berlin-London rate is at the minute 2,200 marks to the pound; the London-New York rate is £1 = 4·4 dollars. A Berlin merchant expending 2,200 marks in purchasing dollars will secure $(2,200 ÷ 510) = $4·03. But a Berlin exchange dealer buying sterling will for 2,200 marks secure £1, with which in London he can buy $4·4. That $4·4 he can immediately sell to the merchant in Berlin for 4·4 × 510 marks = 2,244 marks, thus making 44 marks profit. The Berlin dealer will carry out some such transaction as the following. He will wire his London correspondent to buy thirty thousand dollars at a price up to 500 marks per dollar. From the London correspondent's point of view the deal is acceptable, for it outlines itself thus in his mind:

Selling \$30,000 to Berlin at Mk. 500 per dollar

$$\text{produces in sterling, } \frac{30{,}000 \times 500}{2{,}200} = £6{,}818{\cdot}182$$

$$\text{Cost of buying \$30,000 at } 4{\cdot}44 \text{ is } \frac{30{,}000}{4{\cdot}44} = £6{,}756{\cdot}756$$

Balance, being profit - - £61·426

The London correspondent buys the dollars by telephone and wires the Berlin dealer, who immediately sells them. His calculations are as follows:

Selling \$30,000 at 510 produces -	Mk. 15,300,000
Buying \$30,000 at 500 costs - -	Mk. 15,000,000
Balance, being profit - - -	Mk. 300,000

The transactions might be very much more complicated than this—a whole literature has grown up on this section of the subject alone; but the above example illustrates —clearly, it is hoped—the principles of arbitrage.[1] Speed is the essence of the operation: simultaneously with the transaction of buying dollars in London, the Berlin dealer must sell the equivalent quantity of dollars in Berlin. He dare not allow time to elapse because the rates are likely to fluctuate. Apart from any other causes making for fluctuations, other dealers will be doing the same as he. Exchange arbitrage thus consists of utilizing for profit the different conditions temporarily obtained in other markets, and is a levelling operation which is always tending to make conditions in the various markets uniform.

In the case of a financial house which has branches in two centres, an arbitrage operation such as the above is easier to carry through, for in such a case the operation has to provide a profit margin for one party only. In

[1] The actual profit margins which obtain are usually much smaller than those assumed in the above example.

the above example, if the London correspondent had been the agent or the branch of the Berlin operator, the former could have carried through the transaction even if the dollar rate had meantime fallen lower than 4·44. He could have carried it through at any rate down to 4·40 (2,200 ÷ 500), for down to this rate he could have bought the dollars and remitted them to Berlin at the stipulated price of Mk. 500 per dollar without suffering any loss, thus:

Paid: Cost of $30,000 at 4·40

$$= \frac{30{,}000}{4\cdot40} = £6{,}818\cdot182$$

Received: Value of $30,000 at Mk. 500

= Mk. 15,000,000, worth at 2,200

$$= \frac{£15{,}000{,}000}{2{,}200} = £6{,}818\cdot182$$

Meantime, the principal's margin in Berlin between 500 and 510 would have remained intact.

An operation similar in principle can be carried through in shares or bonds which have a market in more than one country. When exchange rates are stable, the price of, say, Royal Dutch shares in Amsterdam will be a sum in florins, which, when converted into sterling at the current rate of exchange, will be equivalent to the price quoted on the London Stock Exchange. When exchange rates move, the price of these shares will move with them, tending always to the establishment of a common price level in the centres on which they are quoted; but on occasion the adjustment of share prices may lag a little behind the movement of exchange rates. Thus, following a rise in the London-Amsterdam rate, which means a decline in the value of florins, it may happen that Royal Dutch shares are cheaper in Amsterdam than in London, i.e. they can be bought in Amsterdam for a sum in florins, which, when converted into sterling at the now current rate, is fractionally less than the price quoted in London. In these circumstances, a dealer in either centre, or in another centre such as Paris, may be able to snatch a profit by telegraphing a buying order for so many shares to Amsterdam and, as soon as he receives the reply wire advising that the purchase has been made, selling them in London. This operation would itself tend to raise the price in Amsterdam and to depress it in London, and so to establish a new price level common to both centres.

Another issue which should be explained is that of the rate applied in converting into sterling legal damages assessed abroad in a foreign currency.

The decline in the value of the rupee led in 1921 to unexpected and unpleasant results for British exporters to India. A number of Indian importers, upset by the general decline in prices which had occurred since they had placed their orders in 1920—a decline intensified for them by the drop in the value of the rupee—and themselves perhaps not uninfluenced by political propaganda, repudiated their contracts and refused to take up the goods they had bought. Actions claiming damages for breach of contract were brought in Indian courts by British exporters, and substantial damages were awarded. The damages were assessed in the only currency in which an Indian court could assess them—in rupees. The actual payment, however, being made to persons in England, had to be made in sterling, which the defendants would have to purchase and remit. The question therefore arose: At what rate were the rupee damages to be converted into sterling? At the rate ruling on the day when the breach of contract, in respect of which the damages were awarded, took place; or at the rate ruling on the day when judgment was delivered? Between these two dates the rupee had declined in value in terms of sterling. The second date would therefore mean the payment to the successful plaintiffs of a lesser sterling amount than the first. Naturally the English plaintiffs argued for the first rate, the Indian defendants for the second.

Unfortunately for the English plaintiffs, some cases had already been decided in the English courts,[1] in which the rule was laid down that the rate at which damages, awarded in one country to plaintiffs domiciled in another, were to be converted was the rate ruling on the date of judgment. These cases were King's Bench cases, and therefore without the authority attaching to an Appeal case; but the rule was laid down sufficiently clearly to induce the English plaintiffs to accept the Indian defendants' views without taking the matter further.

Into the legal grounds for the King's Bench decisions in question it is unnecessary to go. It may, however, be remarked that the practical effect of these decisions was inequitable, in that they brought about a state of affairs in which a party to a contract for goods, of which the price had declined before delivery could be made, might find it cheaper to refuse to take the goods and have damages awarded against him than to take up the goods; because the damages awarded against the defaulter were automatically diminished, at the time he had to pay them, by the decline in value of the currency in which they were assessed. It might be, that is, more profitable to break a contract than to perform it, a state of things which has induced some buyers to break contracts or to refuse to take up goods unless extortionate allowances were made by the sellers.

[1] *Di Ferdinando* v. *Simon Smits & Co.* (L.R., 1920, Vol. II, K.B. & P., Part VIII) was the chief of these cases.

PART III—EXCHANGE, TRADE, PRICES

CHAPTER VIII

THE BALANCE OF TRADE

WE can now examine the various factors which cause the fluctuations in rates of exchange. These factors are the same in kind to-day as they were before the war, although very different in degree. They may be grouped under six headings, as follows:

(1) Balance of indebtedness.
(2) Rates of interest.
(3) Political events or rumours with financial reactions.
(4) Speculation.
(5) Loans and credits.
(6) Inflation of currency and credit.

So far as No. 3 is concerned, very little need be said. There have been plenty of examples. One may recall the fluctuations in the Anglo-American Exchange at the time the American Senate was discussing the Peace Treaty, when the exchange went alternately up and down according as it was believed that the Senate would or would not ratify the Treaty. There is a still more striking example in the case of Upper Silesia. One of the greatest of the sudden collapses of the German mark began with a slump of 100 to 200 points, on the arrival in Berlin of the news that this country had agreed to the enforcement of the decision which took a large part of Upper Silesia from Germany and gave it to Poland. The reason was that Silesia is an important mining and industrial area and its loss enormously diminished Germany's wealth and productive ability.

Again, so far as No. 4 is concerned, very little need be

said. It is quite evident that when the mark is declining, people who think it is going to decline still further will sell forward, i.e. if the mark is at 800, a man will sell, and buy in when the exchange is at 1,100. The fact that he sells at 800 itself tends to bring the value of the mark down, and when he buys in at 1,100, the mere fact of his buying causes the mark to go up.

The other factors need more detailed analysis.

No. 1, The balance of indebtedness, is made up of five sub-factors:

(*a*) The visible balance of trade.
(*b*) Invisible exports and imports, such as shipping and insurance services, banking, and acceptance services.
(*c*) Interest on capital invested abroad.
(*d*) Payments arising out of social intercourse.

(*b*) is simple. It is quite clear that if goods from the United States of America to the West Indies are carried in a British ship, and payment for the freight is made in London, the effect will be to increase *pro tanto* the demand for sterling on the part of the shippers, who will have to expend dollars to buy the sterling.

It is also quite clear when the accepting house in London financed the shipment of tea from Canton to Milan, it took a commission for doing so, and the use of these acceptance facilities has therefore increased the demand *pro tanto* for sterling.

(*c*) Suppose a municipality in Brazil raises a loan in this country by offering bonds for subscription. In due course it comes to pay the interest on them. That interest has to be paid either in sterling or in milreis. If in sterling, it means that the municipality has to go into the foreign exchange market and buy sterling, which means an increase in the demand for sterling. If on the other hand the interest is to be paid in milreis, it means that when the bondholders here receive their dividends in milreis they sell them, thus putting more milreis on the market; in other words, the milreis becomes cheaper. In the past, this country used to draw tribute from all over the world in this way, because in North and South America, and in fact practically all over the world, railways and large undertakings were to a large extent financed by British capital. This is no longer the case to the same extent, because during the war we were compelled to sell a large portion of our best securities in America in order to raise money there.

(*d*) When an English honeymoon couple go to Italy, they have to buy lire to meet their expenses, and that causes the demand for lire, on the part of people who pay for it in sterling, to increase. Similarly, remittances from Irish and Italians in America to people at home cause a demand for sterling or lire on the part of people who buy these currencies with dollars.

(*a*) This is rather more complicated. The visible balance of trade can of course always be gauged from the Board of Trade returns, which give statistics of imports and exports. The complications arise because not merely does the balance of trade affect the exchanges, but the exchanges themselves have a counter-effect on the balance of trade. Both factors are working at the same time; both are causes, and both are effects. We have to consider separately the effect of each on the other.

The Effect of the Balance of Trade on Exchange Rates.—Clearly, as between country "A" and country "B," an excess of imports over exports in the case of "A" means that "A" will have to accept more bills than it draws; therefore, other things being equal, bills on "A" will be more plentiful than bills on "B," and therefore the price for bills on "A" will be cheaper than the price for bills on "B." We know that the rate on which bankers issue their foreign drafts is determined by the price at which they can buy bills on the country in question, and therefore they will issue drafts on "A" at a cheaper price than bills on "B." That simply means that "A's" rate of exchange will be unfavourable as compared with "B."

In the reverse case, where exports exceed the imports, the same reasoning applies in the reverse direction. In this case, "A's" rate of exchange will be favourable, and "B's" unfavourable.

Such is the reasoning, but these results will only be seen if other things have been equal all along, i.e. if the various other factors, (*b*), (*c*), (*d*), and (*e*), and (2), (3), (4), (5), and (6) have remained unchanged. If for example a country's export trade increased enormously, but at the same time it depreciated its currency very heavily by the issue of paper money, the rates would not go in its favour.[1] All our reasoning is based on the assumption that other things remain equal.

When we come to consider *the counter-effect of the rates of exchange on the balance of trade*, the reasoning is more difficult, for the reason that we have to deal with both the immediate and the secondary effect.

The Immediate Effect.—Take the case where the rate of exchange between "A" and "B" moves in "A's" favour. That will mean that the price of "A's" currency in terms of "B's" will go up in value: in other words, that the prices quoted by merchants in country "A" are increased automatically to their buyers in "B." If the pound one day is worth 50 francs and the rate moves in favour of England, making the rate 51 francs, and the prices charged by merchants in England remain unchanged, the Frenchman will have to pay 51 francs for an article for which yesterday he was paying 50. The effect is evidently that English export trade will be restricted, because there are always a number of people working on a margin. The buyer may be able to afford an article

[1] See the example of Belgium in 1920, quoted in Chapter XII, p. 141.

at 50 francs, but cannot do so at 51 francs; in that case, he does not buy, simply because the rate of exchange has moved in England's favour. Therefore the result of the exchange rates moving in a country's favour is to check the export trade of that country. Following the same line of reasoning conversely, if the rate of exchange goes against England, the effect will be to cheapen English prices to Frenchmen and thereby to increase England's export trade.

So far we have been dealing with immediate effects only. They have led us to the conclusion that an appreciating exchange is a hindrance to the export trade, and a depreciating exchange an advantage to the export trade. And such effects occurred in actual fact in the case of Germany and France, where a constantly depreciating exchange in fact provided an artificial stimulus to the export trade.

But evidently these effects are not the only or the ultimate ones. If a depreciating exchange increases a country's export trade, then clearly during the years following the war the countries with the biggest exports should be Russia, Poland, and Austria. If, again, Germany deliberately depressed the exchange during those years, in order to pull up her export trade, as some newspapers never tire of repeating, it is extraordinary that this method of competition never occurred to her or to anyone else before 1914; and still more extraordinary that neither we nor any other industrial nations have followed her example. There were constant attempts by the German Government and by German financiers to get loans to restore the exchange: apparently, in spite of the artificial stimulus given to the export trade, no one either in England, in the U.S., or on the Continent really believes that lasting benefit is conferred on a country by a depreciating exchange. The explanation of this apparent contradiction is found in the secondary effects of a depreciating exchange.

The Secondary Effect.—A depreciating exchange means that while exports are made cheaper imports are made dearer. In the case of a manufacturing country, the imports consist chiefly of food and raw materials. A depreciating exchange means an increase in the price of food and raw materials, and therefore an increase in the cost of production. To what extent it raises the cost of production will depend upon a number of things. If there is a depreciation of 25 per cent. in the exchange, it does not necessarily mean that the cost of production will go up 25 per cent. They will go up less or more according to the proportion of food and raw materials imported, the ratio which in any given case the cost of imported raw material bears to the total cost of the finished article in question, and the extent to which salary- and wage-earners are able to force up their remuneration to meet increasing prices. What is certain is that the cost of production will go up. The process is somewhat as follows. When the exchange first depreciates it is a benefit to manufacturers. They are able to raise prices in terms of their own currency to the extent to which the exchange has depreciated without making them dearer to the foreigner. At these new prices they can sell stocks manufactured under the old lower costs of production and pocket the difference. The advantage continues so long as their old stocks last. New goods have to be manufactured out of such stocks of raw material bought at the old prices as remain, and when these are exhausted, out of new stocks bought at the higher prices due to the depreciated exchange. Wages meantime are rising, but in general more slowly than prices, and salaries more slowly than wages. Complications are introduced by the questions as to how quickly raw materials and food produced in the country itself rise in price, and how far rail freights lag behind. But broadly speaking the following would seem to be true. So long as the old stocks of raw materials last, the depreciated exchange still puts a margin into the pockets of manufacturers. Even when they have become exhausted, wages and salaries will in all probability not have risen in the same proportion as prices. To the extent that they will fall short, the advantage to the manufacturer remains, though it may be offset by the friction and strikes to which the readjustment of wages is likely to give rise. Ultimately, assuming the depreciation of the exchange to have stopped, a new equilibrium of prices and wages is reached, and the depreciated exchange ceases to be of benefit to the manufacturer, save in so far as real wages and salaries, i.e. remuneration measured in terms of what it will buy, have been permanently lowered by the failure of wage and salary rates to rise in the same ratio as prices.

It is well to be clear on this last point, that the benefit to the industrialists is mainly obtained, not necessarily by their own desire, out of the pockets of the wage-earners, salary-earners, and fixed income-receiving classes of their own country. The incomes of the first rise relatively slowly, those of the second still more slowly, and those of the third not at all. Export prices rise immediately the exchange depreciates, and home prices follow them. Export prices do not necessarily rise to the same extent as the exchange has depreciated—if they did, the depreciation would not be a stimulus to the export trade. Home prices, again, do not necessarily rise to the same extent as export prices; the limitation of the home buying power and governmental regulation, etc., tend to keep them lower.[1] It remains true, however, that the benefit to the export trade conferred by a depreciating exchange is attained mainly at the cost of the middle and working-classes.[2] These are the people who have paid the artificial

[1] See Chapter XIII as to the gap between home and export prices, especially p. 153.

[2] For a comparison of the rises of (a) prices, (b) wages, and (c) salaries, in Germany, concurrently with the decline in value of the mark, see p. 164, footnote.

premium put on the German export trade by the decline of the mark.

It may be added that a portion of the premium is paid by speculators who have bought marks; but as against this are other speculators who have sold marks forward.

Subject to these considerations, a depreciating exchange is an advantage to the export trade, but it is a lasting advantage only so long as it continues to depreciate. In other words, the benefit is that, not of a depreciated exchange, but of a depreciating exchange.[1]

But the examples of Poland, Austria, Russia and especially Germany show that a constantly depreciating exchange ceases at some point to be a benefit even to the export trade by reason of its disastrous effects on the economic life of the country as a whole. At what point it is impossible to say theoretically; certainly the point varies in the case of different countries, according, *inter alia*, to the degree to which it is industrial, to the strength of its organized workers, to the extent to which it is self-sufficing in regard to food and raw materials. The history of Germany in 1923 threw light on this question, and illustrated the disaster into which a continually depreciating exchange leads an industrial country. A detailed consideration of what happened in the case of the paper mark [2] is best postponed until we have in detail dealt with Inflation [3]; here we may anticipate by saying that a constantly depreciating exchange ultimately upsets the economic life of a country—and, if the country in question is industrialized, the political life also—to such an extent that organized competitive production and selling abroad becomes impossible. In Germany depreciation brought about a state of things in which not only did export and home trade become possible only by the use of foreign currencies in place of the mark, but the whole fabric of society began

[1] Mr. F. W. Hirst, in "Common Sense," appears to have been the first to draw the distinction clearly in this form.

[2] See Chapter XIV. [3] See Chapter XII.

to break up. Social revolution was avoided only by action taken by the Government, an essential part of which consisted in the creation of a new and stable currency, which possessed none of the "advantages" of a depreciating currency.

We may sum up the conclusions in outline as follows:

(1) The following generalizations are subject to the disturbing influence of tariffs, import and export prohibitions and restrictions, subsidies, etc.

(2) A depreciated exchange exercises its full benefit on the export trade only so long as stocks of manufactured goods last.

(3) The benefit is obtained by industrialists and merchants at the expense mainly of wage- and salary-earners and people with fixed incomes in their own country.

(4) In this sense it remains beneficial, though to a less degree, so long as stocks of raw material last.

(5) After these two kinds of stocks are exhausted, it is only beneficial until wages and salaries have risen in proportion to prices.

(6) When a new equilibrium of wages, salaries, and prices has been set up, the benefits disappear entirely, except in so far as real wages and salaries may have been permanently lowered, unless the exchange continues to depreciate.

(7) The foregoing benefits are liable to be offset by (*a*) the industrial friction, (*b*) financial difficulties, (*c*) the social and political complications which a depreciating exchange brings in its train.

In the case of a continually depreciating exchange, there is a point at which the factors mentioned under (7) are brought to such a pitch of strength by the exhaustion of internal, and the situation of external, purchasing power, that it ceases to be a benefit even to the export trade, and becomes dangerous to political, social, and economic stability.

CHAPTER IX

LOANS AND CREDITS

WE next have to consider the fourth of the six factors which influence exchange rates: international loans and credits. Such loans and credits may be either private or public. It may be for example that a merchant in Brazil seeks accommodation in London, or it may be that the Brazilian Government floats a loan in London. We may take a case which combines the features of both in order to show how it works: the case of a Brazilian municipality raising a loan in London through a London financial house. The loan may be made in one of three forms. In the first place it may be made through an issuing house, i.e. one of those houses which specialize in placing foreign bonds on the market. The house sells the bonds on behalf of the municipality, people here will subscribe for and receive the bonds, paying the issuing house sterling therefor, and the latter places the money to the credit of the municipality in a London joint-stock bank. Let us say the loan has been raised in order to build a local tramway. The contract for rolling stock, rails, overhead, etc., is placed by the municipality with a well-known British firm. When the goods are ready to be shipped, the municipality instructs the bank which holds its funds to pay the amount of the suppliers' invoice against shipping documents. The effect of the raising of the loan has been to enable the Brazilian municipality to pay for the British manufactures it requires by utilizing British credit facilities. Another way in which the same end might be attained would be by way of a merchant bank. In this instance one of the London merchant bankers agrees with a Brazilian municipality to accept bills drawn upon themselves up to a certain amount. The material is ordered, the contractors draw on the merchant bankers, and the latter pay. In a third instance the loan may be issued through an accepting house: in this case the accepting house gives authority to the municipality to draw upon themselves up to a certain amount. In this case the credit is a blank credit. The municipality have the right to draw on the accepting house up to let us say £10,000. When the material is shipped, the amount the municipality has to pay through its London agents is £8,500. The agents draw £9,000, the accepting house accept the bill, the agents discount it with a London bank, and pay the suppliers out of the balance thereby created.

In all three cases, the effect is that a Brazilian purchaser gets goods for which at the time he pays out of funds lent to him for the purpose by people in London. As a result, he is indebted to people in England, either bondholders, merchant bankers, or an accepting house. The effect of these credit operations clearly is that the municipality will not have to go into the foreign exchange market and buy sterling bills, whereas if it had not had credit, it would have had to do so. In the ordinary way the municipality would have had to spend milreis in purchasing sterling in order to pay the contractors; as it is, they have not had to expend milreis at all. There is therefore less of a demand from Brazil for sterling than there would otherwise have been: the effect of the issuing of this loan is to keep the Brazilian exchange more favourable to Brazil than it would have been had it not been issued. Exactly the same effect would be produced if instead of the municipality the borrower had been any ordinary merchant in Brazil, or the Brazilian Government itself, desirous perhaps of borrowing money from our Government to pay for warships which were being built for them in the shipyards of Great Britain. To generalize, the effect of the giving of credits is to tend to make the exchange favourable to the country which gets the credit.

When the time comes for the interest to be paid on the loan, the effect on the exchanges is exactly opposite. The interest on the bonds may be payable either in sterling or milreis, but the effect will be the same in either case. If payable in sterling, the municipality will have to buy sterling bills in order to create a balance for itself in London out of which it can pay the bondholders. That means the demand from Brazil for sterling bills will be greater than before, and the price of them will rise. If the interest is payable in milreis, it means that a number of bondholders in England will receive drafts in milreis, which they will sell to their banks, and the banks will sell on the foreign exchange market. Therefore there will be a larger supply of milreis than before, and the price of milreis will be less. The exchange will tend to go against Brazil just as in the case when the interest was payable in sterling.

The creation of loans will favour the exchange of the debtor country. The payment of interest will favour the exchange of the creditor country.

The effect of the repayment of the loans in question is similar. In the case of the loans made by the merchant bankers and the accepting house, the period of the loan would be relatively short, and the loan known as a short-dated credit; in the case of the bonds, it would probably be a long-dated loan. In either case, the effects of repayment on the exchange are the same in principle as when the interest had to be paid, i.e. the municipality once more had to go into the market and buy sterling in order to repay the English creditors.

Before the war, London financial houses did a very great deal of this sort of business. American, Australian, Canadian, and South American municipalities, railroads, and public utility companies all made a habit of financing their requirements in London. The commission obtained on this business was an element of considerable profit to this country, and the interest obtained from capital invested abroad was an item which swelled the income of this country to the tune of about 400 millions annually. Now, an important part of that has gone, because the best of our foreign securities were sold during the war in the United States. New York, again, has become a better centre than London for raising loans, because the resources of the United States were greatly increased by the war, whereas those of Britain were greatly diminished, and the dollar has since the war possessed that certain convertibility into gold which before the war was the property of the pound alone and which the pound lacked between 1914 and 1925. The financing of, e.g. Canadian public and private requirements, i.e. municipal loans and the capital issues of limited companies, has largely passed from London to New York.

The floating of loans and the giving of credits was the means whereby Britain assisted her allies financially during the war, and whereby the U.S. assisted Britain. It was the means whereby, before the U.S. entered the war, the dollar exchange was fixed at the figure of 4·76½, or, as it was called, "pegged." The principle was that payments for food and munitions supplied by U.S. firms to this country were made out of dollar funds raised in the United States, so that no dollars had to be bought, and therefore these British purchases did not for the time being produce any effect on the exchange. The details of this pegging are worthy of examination, as they are very instructive in regard to the operation of this part of exchange machinery.

Towards the end of 1914, the decline of the export trade of the Allied belligerent countries and their necessity to import, at a time when their resources were being progressively devoted to the war, caused the neutral, and especially the American, exchanges to move against them. In September, 1915, the dollar was down to 4·75 and it was clear that, in the absence of preventive measures, it would decline further by reason of the huge payments necessitated by imports of food and munitions. It had become evident that a war policy based on unlimited military commitments would require, in order to pay for imports of food and munitions in the absence of any considerable exports, the selling of oversea investments and the creation of a foreign debt. The alternative was to limit English military participation and to rely, apart from the very considerable armies already raised at that time, on naval and economic means. The former course was chosen. Loans were raised in the United States and foreign investments were sold in New York to provide funds. By this means the necessity of buying dollars to pay for food and munitions was avoided for the time and the dollar remained at the figure of 4·76½.

At first, British loans in America were raised in somewhat the same manner as, in the imaginary example set out earlier, the Brazilian municipality raised its loan in England. They were raised through the firm of J. P. Morgan & Co., and out of the funds so provided, payment was made for British imports of food and munitions. As time went on, and the destruction of the belligerent countries' resources became evident to the neutral world, a feeling arose in the U.S. that such loans should not be issued without some security behind them, and a regulation was issued to that effect. This necessitated that when England raised loans in the U.S. (we are still dealing of course with the period prior to the entry of the U.S. into the war) collateral securities had to be deposited. This gave rise to what was known in England as the "Dollar Securities Scheme." Residents in England were invited to surrender to the British Treasury securities of various kinds in the Treasury circulars. The Treasury promised either to return them the securities or to pay the owners their market value; in the meantime the owners would receive the interest due, but the Treasury had the right to dispose of the securities as it thought fit. The securities covered by that scheme were such as the U.S. financial community would accept as security for loans, and consisted, broadly speaking, of the choicest of the American (U.S., South American, and Canadian) bonds held in England. Finding that the voluntary appeal to owners of listed securities to surrender them did not have the effect of mobilizing all the securities available, the Treasury in 1916 instituted a penal income tax on the income from securities not handed to the Treasury. Finally, the handing over of the listed securities was made compulsory. The securities so obtained by the Treasury were either sold in New York or deposited as collateral securities for loans in the U.S. It was when England was approaching a point at which loans had been issued to the full extent to which the Americans were willing to lend on the security of these bonds that Mr. Bonar Law made his famous declaration, early in 1917, that "our resources are not unlimited." What would have been the course of events had not the U.S. entered the war at this point is of course one of those "might-have-beens" which fascinate the historical imagination. The considerations at issue in the first months of 1917 were not merely financial, but economic; unless the food, raw materials, and munitions which America alone could supply in adequate quantities could be obtained, the war would have had to be ended. Credits could not be obtained without security, and there was no more security to give, with the possible exception of the cession of the West Indian Islands. Without credits, the sterling used in purchasing dollars would have declined rapidly in value, and with every decline the imports would automatically have become dearer. As it was clear that only by virtue of a greatly superior supply of food and munitions (as well as men) could Germany be defeated, the ending of the war by a negotiated peace could not, it would seem, have been long delayed.

The entry of the U.S. into the war solved the problem

by altering the manner in which loans in America were raised. Hitherto the money had come from private individuals in the U.S.; henceforth the loans were made by the U.S. Government These loans were made chiefly to Britain, Britain re-lending the money to her Allies.

The U.S. Government paid U.S. manufacturers and grain exporters for the goods and food supplied to the European belligerents, debiting therefor the British Government, which in turn debited its Allies in the cases where the goods and food were supplied to them. The position in 1922, when the debt position as between Britain and the U.S. was clarified, was broadly speaking that Britain owed the United States about 978 millions, and was owed a larger sum by her former Allies and her Dominions.[1]

The dollars exchange remained at the figure of 4·76½, there being nothing to move it, until March, 1919, when it was "unpegged," i.e. the British Treasury announced that no further steps would be taken to stabilize it.

In the case of the Central Powers, which for practical purposes consisted of Germany, the problem was different. Germany was, save in certain limited directions, barred from export and import, and conducted the war from her own resources. The problems of the foreign exchanges only arose in the case of the limited directions in which export and import was possible—Holland, Sweden, Denmark, and, for a time, Rumania. In these cases credits were arranged, and liquidated by the export of stipulated goods, such as coal.[2]

Connected with the subject of the influence of international loans on the exchanges is that of the relationship between the stock market and the exchanges. The purchase of the securities of a foreign country is in effect

[1] For details, and a statement of the position in early 1926, see Chapter XVIII.

[2] Details are given in Helferrich: "Der Weltkrieg" (IIer Band, "Vom Kriegsausbruch bis zum uneingeschränkten U-Bootkrieg").

a loan to that country. When the British Treasury sold dollar securities in the United States, Americans were in effect repaying former loans. When a British investor buys French war-loan or shares in a Spanish mine, he is in effect putting money into France or Spain. If the securities he buys were previously held in the country of origin, the former holder will have to be paid in francs or pesetas, and these will ultimately have to be bought by sterling. If the securities purchased were already held in Britain, the purchaser is in effect renewing a previous loan; if the purchaser, instead of being an Englishman, had been a Frenchman or a Spaniard, the securities would have been sent back to France or Spain, and the purchaser there would have had to buy sterling in order to pay for them. In the first case, a demand from London for francs or pesetas is set up which did not exist before; in the second case, a potential demand for sterling is prevented from coming into existence. The effect in either case is to tend to influence the exchange against sterling, i.e. against the purchasing country. The position may be viewed as an import of securities [1] into Britain, which like other imports has to be paid for and therefore tends to send the exchange against the importing country.

The stock market and the foreign exchanges act and react on each other. If the tendency is for, e.g., Brazilian securities to go up in value, then the value of Brazilian currency will tend to go up with them, i.e. the number of milreis to be surrendered for one pound will go down. The reason is that a rise in the price indicates the activities of buyers on this side, who will require milreis to remit in payment for the securities newly absorbed by the English market. Similarly, if the Brazilian exchange is unfavourable to Brazil, quotations for Brazilian securities worth so many milreis will naturally tend to go down. In the ordinary way, this would be a good time to buy

[1] The conception is that of Mr. Hartley Withers.

Brazilian securities, and such purchases, in their turn, would tend to set the exchange right.

From 1919 onwards the low exchange rates of a good many continental countries have caused a good deal of capital to flow into them by way of the purchase of their industrial securities. The price of German, Austrian, Hungarian, Czech, and Polish industrial securities advanced on the heels of their falling exchanges, but did not always keep up with them. When it fell behind, these securities looked cheap to foreign buyers, and capital flowed in accordingly. Thus English and French capital went into Austria, Hungary, and Czecho-Slovakia; French capital into Poland; American, English and Dutch capital into Germany. Later the losses sustained by English industrialists in the slump following 1920, together with the evident instability of Central Europe, reacted against this investment of capital abroad. The greater degree of stability attained on the Continent during 1924-1925 caused a fresh inflow of English and American capital.

Another interesting illustration of the relation between the exchanges and the stock market is supplied by the following advice given in May, 1920, by a well-known firm of investment bankers in London to those of their clients who had sums on deposit in France in francs, representing money that was owing to them. These clients had left the money in France hoping that the exchange would from France's point of view improve, but had at length come to the opinion that no such improvement was likely. They were accordingly faced with the question how best to deal with these franc balances without absolutely cutting the loss by exchanging them for sterling at the then ruinous rate of exchange. They were advised by the investment bankers "to invest the amount in francs in some good foreign Government Bond, quoted in Paris, interest and capital of which are payable not only in francs, but in sterling, and possibly some other currency, such as Brazilian

Government or Argentine Government Bonds or Stocks. Of course, the franc quotations of these Bonds bear some relation to the present depreciated value of the franc, but by converting francs into such Bonds, the holder insures himself against any further depreciation, secures a high rate of interest (payable in francs or sterling as he desires) on the capital outstanding, and gives to his capital mobility, for he can at any time bring the Bonds over to this country, where they can be sold for sterling without being affected by the French rate of exchange ; and at the same time, he retains the possibility of adding to his capital in francs in the event of the quotation of the foreign Bonds rising in Paris."

The reasoning is clear enough. Another recent example of the same process occurred in March, 1926. Uruguayan Central Railway stock appreciated considerably in expectation of an increased dividend. The increase was expected, not because the railway had earned an appreciably greater net profit, but because the Uruguayan peso had improved and become worth so much more in terms of sterling that larger dividend remittances in sterling than before could be made out of the same amount in pesos.

CHAPTER X

THE SILVER EXCHANGES

THE Eastern exchanges are subject to all the ordinary factors governing the movement of exchange rates, named at the beginning of Chapter VIII, and in addition they vary with the price of silver. They are the exchanges of the silver-using countries, and there are therefore in these cases no pars of exchange [1] and no gold points. In the last instance, silver, and not gold, is shipped for what it will fetch. Purchasing Eastern exchange is really purchasing a claim to silver. Hence these exchanges fluctuate according, not only to the general factors influencing exchange fluctuations which we have examined, but also according to the price of silver, in terms of gold. The price of silver plus or minus shipping charges roughly fixes the rate above and below which the Eastern exchanges will not go. That statement of course is subject to the very important exception of India, which is governed by special conditions. During and for some time after the war, the price for silver went up very considerably, and the Eastern exchanges appreciated accordingly. The rise in the price of silver was due to both the decrease in the supply and the increase in the demand. The decrease in the supply, due directly or indirectly to the war, can be seen by comparing the figures for the total world production of silver in 1913 and 1918. Between those dates it had declined by something over 18 per cent. The increase in the demand was brought about by various factors, of which we may name three as the chief:

(1) Silver, and of course paper, was required to take the place of gold which went out of circulation in this and other belligerent countries; while the need for silver as

[1] **Except in the case of Japan, where the *yen* is on a gold basis.**

a medium of circulation, independently of its replacing gold, was increased in those parts of the world which were blessed with a British Army of Occupation, such as Egypt and Mesopotamia.

(2) During the war period, India and China absorbed considerable quantities, which was hoarded. The native likes to keep his wealth in the form of silver, just as some people like to keep theirs in the form of jewellery.

(3) The price of silver was sent up by the depreciation of the medium in which the price was being reckoned, e.g. English currency. The decline in the value of English currency during the war was shown, *inter alia*, by the increase in prices: silver is a commodity like everything else, and as the prices of other things went up, so did the price of silver.

The operation of those various factors in raising the price of silver was very marked. In 1914 its price (June 30th) was 26d. per ounce. In October, 1919, the price reached 64d. per ounce; in February, 1920, it went to 89½d. per ounce. We shall find that the increase in the value of the Eastern exchange which took place was roughly parallel. The Chinese tael for example in 1914 averaged 2s. 4d., in October, 1919, it had risen to 6s. 4d., and in February, 1920, to 9s. 3d. The percentage increases were thus:

	Silver	Tael
1914 to Oct., 1919 - -	167	171½
1914 to Feb., 1920 - -	273	296½

from which the close correspondence between the rise in value of silver and of the tael is evident. The same correspondence was observed later in 1920, when the price of silver and the value of the tael declined. During 1920, in fact, the value of the tael fluctuated between 3s. 10½d. and 9s. 3d. The Hong-Kong dollar followed a similar course. The uncertainty which these fluctuations brought into Far Eastern and similarly to the Indian trade is obvious: the enormous rise in the purchasing power of these coins induced purchasers to order goods far in excess of what the market could take. Frequently when the time came for payment, the currencies had declined in value. Sometimes, as in a number of cases in India, the goods were not taken up, and had to be sold for what they would fetch, after having accumulated huge charges for warehousing and interest. However disposed of, they choked the market, and when the slump came in the wake of the price boom of early 1920, they hindered the market's recovery.

Another interesting example of the relation between the price of silver and the exchange values of Eastern currencies, and the connexion of the two with the stock and share market, was observed about the turn of the year 1919–1920, when there was a sensational rise in the shares of one of the large German banks—the Deutsch-Asiatische Bank. The reason was that the bank, as its name suggests, operated largely in China and Japan. The increase in the value of silver brought about an increase in the value of Chinese and Japanese currencies, and that meant an increase in the value of the property and funds owned by the bank; hence the shares of the bank were considered to be of more value.

In India the standard coin is the silver rupee. The position prior to 1920 was that of a gold exchange standard. The rupee was an example of currency that was a sort of "half-way house"[1] between convertibility into gold and non-convertibility. Anyone who had sovereigns in India had the right to change those sovereigns into rupees at the rate of 15 to the pound, but the converse was not true. There was no obligation on the Indian Mint to give sovereigns in exchange for rupees. Before the basis of Indian currency was altered in 1920, the rupee had to contain 165 grains of fine silver. As one ounce of standard silver

[1] The term was applied by Mr. Hartley Withers.

contains 444 grains of fine silver, it follows that one rupee equalled $\frac{165}{444}$ of the price per ounce of standard silver. From that we get Clare's rule [1] for determining the approximate sight exchange of the rupee from the price of standard silver. The rule is: The approximate sight exchange can be got from the price of standard silver by adding $\frac{3}{8}$d. to $\frac{3}{8}$th of the price per ounce of silver. Thus, supposing the price of standard silver to be 40d. per ounce, $\frac{3}{8}$ths of that is 15d., and if we add $\frac{3}{8}$d., we get 1s. 3$\frac{3}{8}$d., which would be the approximate sight exchange when silver is 40d.

The trade balance was nearly always in favour of India. Exports more than counterbalanced imports to such an extent that it provided a surplus over and above all the payments which India had to make, which can be summarized under four headings:

(1) For imports.
(2) For interest on government and railway loans.
(3) For I.C.S. pensions.
(4) For the upkeep of the India Office in London.

The actual machinery by which remittances to and from India are made is also worthy of a brief examination. Remittances to India are made by means of India Council drafts. They are drafts sold in London to merchants who have to remit to India, and consist of bills drawn on the Indian Treasuries and payable at various places in India in rupees. They are obtainable both in the form of deferred transfers and immediate telegraphic transfers. The deferred transfers are cheaper than the telegraphic transfer by, as a rule, $\frac{1}{32}$d. per rupee.[2] The difference represents interest for the period which elapses before the buyer of the deferred transfer, who has paid sterling for it, is credited with the rupees. Remittances in the other direction, i.e. from India to England, are made

[1] "The A.B.C. of the Foreign Exchanges."
[2] Spalding, "Foreign Exchange and Foreign Bills," p. 134.

either by ordinary sterling drafts or by "Reverse Councils." These Reverse Councils are sterling drafts sold by the Indian Government, payable in London ; they are sold when the demand for sterling drafts is large, and pre-war they were sold at a fixed price which was $1/3\frac{29}{32}$d. per rupee. The fact that the Indian Government was always willing to sell Reverse Councils at that fixed rate, determined, as it were, the lower gold point. The means whereby the Indian Government was able to sell Reverse Councils were provided by a gold backing in London, in the form of gold reserves which the Bank of England held in London for the Indian Government. The combination of a trade balance favourable to India and the right to exchange sovereigns into rupees enabled the rupee, although not based on gold, to be maintained at a fixed exchange rate with gold—at the figure of 1s. $3\frac{29}{32}$d.

During and after the war, the increase in the price of silver put the Indian Government in a very difficult position. With the rupee at 16d., the cost of the silver in it to anyone who melted it down would be $16 \times \frac{444}{165}$ per oz. = 43d. per oz. If therefore the price of standard silver went above that figure, then the obvious tendency would be for rupees to be melted down and sold as silver bullion, which would create a recurrent shortage of currency in India ; on the other hand, to coin fresh rupees at the legal rate of 15 per pound when silver was costing so much more would have meant a huge loss to the Indian Government. To get out of that difficulty they adopted three palliative measures and then in 1920 a fourth measure, which amounted to an entire alteration of the basis of Indian currency. The three measures were :

(1) They prohibited the import and export of silver.

(2) They increased the price of council drafts to 2s. 4d., that is, they made the rupee more valuable.

(3) They imported gold at the rate of 11 rupees to the pound and then sold it in India.

The last-named measure amounted in effect to this: they induced the Indian population to invest its wealth in gold. A favourable trade balance and the increase in the price of silver were thus partly offset by India importing gold. As these three measures did not surmount the difficulty, they adopted the fourth measure, which amounted to changing the basis of Indian currency. In February, 1920, when pounds were inconvertible paper currency, the Indian Government fixed a rupee at one-tenth of a gold sovereign. The effect of that decision provided an interesting lesson in exchange economics. Before this alteration a rupee was valued at 2s. 4d.; after being fixed at one-tenth of a gold sovereign, it jumped to 2s. 9d. The jump illustrated the depreciation of the pound. It showed that gold prices were something different to prices in English paper currency. The amount of the jump, practically 18 per cent., represented the amount by which paper prices were higher than gold prices. As a matter of fact, at that time if we had worked out the depreciation of the English pound on the basis of the then price of gold in terms of Bradburys, we should have found that round about 20 per cent. was the actual extent of the depreciation of the paper pound in terms of gold.

The idea underlying the decision to fix the rupee at one-tenth of a gold sovereign was that when sterling recovered its parity with gold, the value of the rupee would have been permanently increased. In effect, however, that reasoning did not hold good. Since that time the rupee has fallen considerably in value. The Indian importer who had the pleasure of seeing the rupee go up to 2s. 4d. and then jump further to 2s. 9d. and was then assured by the Government that the increase in value was to be permanent found that nothing of the sort was the case. That was due to two factors. In the first place, silver did not maintain the price it reached —the price of silver in July, 1922, for example was $35\frac{1}{8}$d. as against $88\frac{1}{4}$d. in February, 1920. That was one cause of the decline in value. The second was that the Indian trade balance went against India. Into the causes of that we cannot here go in detail, but we may name two: one was that India bought heavily following the termination of the war, and of course had to pay for those imports; and another cause was that one of India's largest pre-war markets for tea, Russia, disappeared from the market for an indefinite period. As a result of the swinging-over of the trade balance, and the decline in the price of silver, the Indian rupee slumped very considerably. It was not even maintained at 2s. paper, let alone 2s. gold. In July, 1922, its value measured in terms of the paper pound was 1s. $3\frac{5}{8}$d. Then a recovery set in, as payment for the heavy imports of the boom period was completed and the trade balance went in India's favour again, and the rupee finally steadied at about 1s. 6d. At the present time a commission is again considering the whole question of Indian currency, for as a result of the failure of the attempt to stabilize the exchange value of the rupee at one-tenth of a gold sovereign, the entire Indian currency position is once again being reviewed and a new scheme is expected. In some quarters it is anticipated that the exchange value of the rupee will again be fixed at 1s. 6d.

CHAPTER XI

INTEREST RATES: BANK RATE AND THE EXCHANGES

WE have now to consider the influence of rates of interest on exchange rates. The importance of the interplay of interest rates and exchange rates is that on this interplay depended the whole regulating machinery of British exchange rates. That regulating machinery is bank rate. Bank rate is the rate at which the Bank of England will discount approved bills of exchange of three months' maturity. Bank rate operates to regulate the exchange rates between London and other free gold markets through the interplay which exists between exchange rates and the interest rates ruling in London.

Keeping firmly in mind the fact that the price at which a banker will issue a draft in foreign currency is determined by the price at which he can buy bills in that currency, it is evident that the way in which rates of interest will affect exchange rates is by influencing the price of bills. The organization by means of which bills are exchanged for cash is the money market, and it is therefore necessary to examine in outline its structure and functions. The business of the money market consists in exchanging cash for short period promises to pay. These promises are in the form of bills of exchange. Bills are the commodity in which the money market deals. Ordinary merchants dealing in goods are the producers of bills, as we saw in Chapter IV; the joint-stock banks are the consumers. The intermediaries between the two, the dealers in bills, are the bill-brokers and discount houses. This does not mean that the joint-stock banks do not buy bills direct from the ordinary mercantile holder; they do so buy; but they do so only incidentally, as one only of their many activities. The specialized dealers in bills, the bill-brokers and discount houses on the other hand, do nothing else but buy and sell bills, and from them quotations can always be obtained. The bill-brokers and discount houses, together with the accepting houses or merchant bankers and the London offices of British overseas banks, constitute the " discount market " ; and the discount market, together with the joint-stock banks and the Bank of England, constitutes the money market.

How bills of exchange originate and come into the money market we have already seen in Chapter IV. In the case of the bill drawn by Chung Ling Soo on Steinfelds, it will be remembered that the manager of the Canton branch of a British bank trading overseas made an advance to Chung Ling Soo against the bill before acceptance. When the bill has arrived in London and been accepted by Steinfelds, the London office of the bank, if they do not wish to hold it till maturity, will sell it to a discount house. The difference between the London discount rate and the rate at which the Canton manager made the advance represents profit to the bank. Before dealing with the bill-brokers and discount houses, it will be well to be clear as to the ultimate consumers of bills—the joint-stock banks. Why can the banks be relied on by the bill-brokers to buy bills ? The reason is this : The outstanding considerations in English banking policy are to keep resources liquid and at the same time to earn interest on them. Apart from the general desirability of keeping resources liquid, since a bank's liabilities are payable on demand (current accounts) or at seven days' notice (deposit accounts) there are certain times of the year at which a bank is particularly in need of ready cash. One such time is the end of December, when, as we all know, there is a certain amount of " window-dressing " in order that the banks' balance sheets may present a favourable appearance in the sense that there is plenty of ready cash available. Another time the banks require particularly large cash resources is during the months of February and March, when clients are drawing large cheques in order to meet income tax. The banks therefore are faced with the necessity of earning interest on money deposited with them in such a manner that a large proportion of that money can be turned into cash at a moment's notice, or better still, will turn itself automatically into cash within a definite time. The way the bank fulfils these two requirements is by:

(*a*) Investing its money in bills of exchange.
(*b*) Lending money at call or short notice.

A bill of exchange will automatically fall due for payment on a certain date, and if it is a good bill, i.e. has good names upon it, it will automatically turn itself into cash on that date. If therefore a bank knows it will require a large amount of cash by a certain date, it buys in from bill-brokers or discount houses a sufficient number of bills of exchange maturing on that date. It thereby secures the certainty of having cash on the date when cash is required and also earns the difference between the face value of the bill, which it receives on maturity, and the amount the bank itself gave for the bill. An example will show that a bank buying a bill with good names on it is sure to make a moderate but certain profit. Take the case of the three months' bill for £100 mentioned in Chapter IV, which the bank, deducting the market rate of discount for three months' trader bills, 5½ per cent. per annum, bought for £98 12s. 6d. The money employed by the banker in buying it is money deposited with him by a customer, on which he has to pay the customer interest. On the same day that trade bills were quoted in the Press at 5 per cent. to 5½ per cent., the Bankers' deposit rate was quoted at 3½ per cent. per annum. The banker has to pay interest at 3½ per cent. per annum on the money deposited with him, which he employed in buying the bill. The sum which the banker had to expend is therefore £98 12s. 6d. plus interest on that at $3\frac{1}{2}$ per cent. for three months:

$$= £98\ 12s.\ 6d.\ \text{plus}\ \frac{98{\cdot}625 \times 7 \times 1}{100 \times 2 \times 4}$$
$$= £98\ 12s.\ 6d.\ \text{plus}\ 17s.$$
$$= £99\ 9s.\ 6d.$$

As his total incomings, i.e. the face value of the bill when it matures, are £100, he makes a profit of 10s. 6d. on a transaction of £100 in three months. His profit is at the rate of 2 per cent. per annum.

In fact, his profit is greater, for he would not have to pay interest on the whole of the money. A large quantity of the funds at a banker's disposal do not consist of money placed with him on deposit, but of current accounts, on which he does not pay interest at deposit rate. So in point of fact his expenses are not equal to the figure stated and his profit is correspondingly greater. Moreover, a banker cannot make a loss on the transaction, for deposit rates are normally lower than discount rates. For the banker, such a transaction—always assuming a good bill, and bankers touch no others—shows a moderate and certain profit, and assures that, on a definite date, so much of his assets will automatically turn itself into cash. It is of course true that if discount rates went down and the banker desired to sell the bill, he might have to sell it for less than he gave for it. But banks do not buy bills for resale, but by way of short-dated investment for their funds, and customarily hold them till maturity.

We also said that banks employ a proportion of their funds in loans at call or at seven days' notice. These loans are made to a large extent to the bill-brokers from whom the banks customarily buy their bills of exchange, and such loans are known collectively, as "loans to the short loan market," which is so called because the period of the loan is short. The banks also make short loans to stockbrokers and other parties, but in the greatest measure their loans at call and short notice are made to bill-brokers. It is natural to ask: Why do not the banks buy direct from the people who have bills to sell, instead of financing bill merchants to do the business for them? The answer is that there is just as much or as little justification for the existence of a bill-broker as there is for that of any other middleman. Bill-brokers who specialize in inland bills make it their business to have in their portfolios bills of the kind and maturity which the banks favour. Those who specialize in foreign currency bills make it their business to know what people want, e.g. kroner bills, and what people have kroner bills to sell. The case is similar to that of a dealer in commodities, who makes his living by knowing which people have his particular line of commodities to sell, and which people want to buy. He does the business cheaper than the banks could do it themselves with the same degree of efficiency. If a bank had its own official to buy bills he would have to be a high-salaried man with a wide knowledge of the bill market, he would have to have his clerks and typists, and he would have to employ the bank's capital. In the end, he would cost the bank more than does the commission or margin paid to the bill-broker. So well recognized is this fact, that bankers not only buy bills from the bill-brokers, but themselves finance the bill-brokers. The major part of a bill-broker's business is done on money borrowed from the banks against the deposit of bills or bonds as security; and the bill-brokers make their living by having in their portfolios bills of just the kind and just the maturity which they know the banks will want. On occasion the bill-broker works entirely on commission. In the ordinary way, his profits are mainly derived from the margin between bill and money rates,[1]

[1] See lecture by D. Spring Rice on the money market printed in the "Bankers' Magazine," issue of March, 1922.

i.e. between the rate of discount which he deducts from a bill when paying cash for it and the rate of interest which he has paid to the bank for the loan of that cash. In addition there is of course the interest on his capital, which is in the form of investments which can be pledged as security for the loans he requires.[1]

The price at which bills are sold is quoted in terms of the rate of discount that is deducted from them, and that rate is known as the market rate. This is the rate on which we have to fix our attention. It is only one of a number of rates of interest obtaining in the money market. These rates are more or less connected. Bank rate is one of them. Bank rate and market rate do not necessarily vary with one another; the exact relations between them we shall examine later on. Deposit rate is another, being the rate of interest allowable by the joint-stock and merchant banks on balances deposited with them subject to withdrawal at seven days' notice. Deposit rate varies in an upward or downward direction with bank rate. The rate of interest on loans to bill-brokers is generally, but not always, a fraction higher than deposit rate. The rate of interest charged by bill-brokers on bills, i.e. the market rate of discount, is necessarily a little higher than the rate of interest which bill-brokers pay on their loans from the banks.

The factors which determine the market rate of discount, i.e. the price of bills in terms of cash, are more complicated than those which determine the prices of commodities in terms of cash, for not only the supply of bills, but also the supply of cash at the disposal of the short loan market, is constantly fluctuating. The causes of the fluctuations in the supply of cash in the money market cannot be gone into here: obviously they will largely derive from the state of trade and of the investment market and from taxation.

So far as the fluctuations in the supplies of bills are

[1] See lecture by D. Spring Rice on the money market printed in the "Bankers' Magazine," issue of March, 1922.

concerned, we have first of all to distinguish between commercial bills and finance bills.[1] The fluctuations in supply mainly affect finance bills and only secondarily commercial bills. So far as the latter are concerned, it is evident that the price that has to be paid for financial accommodation in the money market will not immediately affect the supply of commercial bills that come forward for discounting, because these commercial bills will be simply the results of transactions entered into a considerable time ago, and entered into by merchants whose profits normally are large enough to enable them not to be vitally interested in marginal variations in the rate at which their bills will have to be discounted. A change in money market conditions will not in the first instance affect the supply of commercial bills. The change may, as we shall see, affect that supply later on if it continues long enough. But the supply of finance bills is affected very much indeed by conditions in the money market. It is not difficult to see why bills of this kind are much more susceptible to money market influences. The mercantile drawer of a finance bill loses the discount on the bill when he discounts it, he loses the acceptance house's commission, and he loses the interest on the amount for the two days before maturity when he has to put the accepting house in funds. He has therefore to think carefully about the rate at which he can discount the bill before drawing, in order to see whether it is worth his while to pay for the additional accommodation. The less profit he is making on his business, the more carefully he will look at the amount the accommodation costs. It may happen that although these facilities are at his disposal, he refrains from using them, because a marginal increase in discount rates makes it just not worth his while. In other words, the drawing of such bills may depend entirely upon the marginal fluctuations in the market rate of discount.

[1] See Chapter IV.

And if that is true of a mercantile drawer, it would be much more true of a merchant banker in Paris, Berlin, or Stockholm. A merchant banker does not work on a fairly substantial margin of profit, but on a much finer margin. He relies on being able to use the funds which he acquires at a profit only slightly greater than the cost: on being able to lend money at a slightly higher rate than that at which he borrows it. Whether a foreign banker in possession of a number of blank credits with London accepting houses uses them or not will quite definitely be determined by the market rate of discount. It will depend from time to time on the rates at which his London bankers will discount such drafts whether he draws or not. These are primarily the kind of bills we have in mind when we speak of the volume of bills expanding and contracting.

We are now in a position to examine in detail the effect of variations in the market rate of discount on exchange rates. It must be borne in mind that the following reasoning, which applied, with rare exceptions, at all times and to all rates before the war, is now of limited and partial application only. At the moment of writing [1] it applies only as between Britain and those other countries which are free gold markets: the United States, Sweden, Holland, the Union of South Africa, Australia, and New Zealand. Why it does not apply elsewhere, and why it did not apply even in the cases named between 1918 and 1925, will be clear when we have described how the process operates. [2]

Let us assume first a decline in market rate. (1) Other things being equal, a low market rate of discount evidently will encourage the foreigner who has facilities for drawing on accepting houses in London to use them. A merchant banker in New York will, other things being equal, be encouraged by the fact that he can discount drafts cheaply, i.e. sell them in London for something near their face

[1] June, 1926. [2] See Chapter XVII.

value, to bring them into existence, and that reasoning will apply more or less to the bulk of people abroad who have drawing facilities in London. Therefore a volume of sterling bills will be brought into existence which otherwise would not have been created. Sterling bills, being accordingly more numerous, will become cheaper, and the amount of foreign currency to be given for them less; in other words, the exchanges will tend to go against Britain. (2) Again, the various interest rates allowed by the joint-stock and merchant banks move together, and a low market rate of discount implies a low deposit rate. When, therefore, the merchant banker in New York, by drawing as above, provided himself with funds in London, his inclination will be to withdraw them from London to another centre where rates of interest are higher and they can earn more. (3) The same will be true of a large quantity of the balances held in London at the disposal of foreigners. These balances will be remitted abroad by foreign currency drafts, so that a demand for such drafts will be set up.

A low market rate of discount therefore tends to increase the supply of sterling bills and to increase the demand for foreign currency, both of which factors tend to make the exchanges adverse to Britain.

In the case of a high market rate, the reasoning will be reversed. (1) The fact that bills in London cost a good deal to discount will tend to prevent foreigners drawing on London; the tendency will therefore be for the volume of sterling bills to get less, because as they run off they will not be renewed; and as the volume of sterling bills becomes less, the price will go up. That means the exchanges will tend to go in our favour. (2) Again, under the same conditions of a high market rate, foreigners who have sold goods to Britain and been paid in London, will tend to leave their money in London in order to earn the benefit of the high market rate of discount. If a foreign merchant who has sold us goods has no particular use for his money for two or three weeks, he can leave it on deposit with one of the London merchant banks in order to obtain the benefit of the high rates of interest obtaining in London. The tendency therefore will be for foreign creditors to leave their money here instead of having it sent to them; that means that the banks, instead of having to buy foreign currency drafts to remit to these foreign clients, will not have to do so. To that extent there will be less demand for foreign currency drafts, which again means that the value of sterling will go up. (3) Similarly, merchant bankers with balances abroad will send their money here in order to earn the high rates of interest in operation. These balances, it must be remembered, do not consist of investment money; they are floating balances, and they float towards high rates of interest. Once here they can be employed in discounting bills and obtaining the high rate of discount available, or put out on deposit with one of the London discount houses and earn the high deposit rates that will normally accompany a high market rate. The effect of (1) is to diminish the volume of sterling bills in existence; the effect of (2) is to diminish the demand for foreign currency; the effect of (3) is to set up a demand abroad for sterling drafts: francs, dollars, and marks are used to buy sterling drafts. In all these three ways the raising of the market rate of discounts operates to turn the exchanges in our favour.

The reactions so far described as the result of market rate being raised or lowered have all related to finance bills. It is this class of bills which are in the first instance affected by changes in market rate. But a long-continued low or high market rate also affects the supply of commercial bills. In the case of a long-continued low rate it tends to increase the supply of commercial bills; a long-continued high rate, to diminish it. In the case of the low rate, a buyer of commodities who requires accommodation can get it easily, for not only can he discount bills cheaply, but also a low market rate implies that other rates of interest are low too. In other words, the merchant will get his bank overdrafts cheaper. That state of easy accommodation continued over a long period will encourage importers. This means the coming into existence of a number of bills drawn on London by suppliers abroad, which would not have come into existence had it not been for the fact that imports were particularly easy to finance. A low market rate, therefore, over a period of time, will tend to increase the volume also of commercial bills, and thereby to turn the exchanges further against us.

To that statement there is an exception. If the long-continued supply of cheap money is due to the fact that there is very little business doing, because confidence has been shaken, perhaps by some big failure, or by political conditions, then it may be that the absence of business confidence will discourage buyers more than the cheap money will encourage them and the excess of commercial bills will not come into existence. Such has been the condition of things on various occasions since the slump came in the second half of 1920, e.g. in July, 1922.

A long-continued high market rate makes accommodation dear and hence discourages buyers. Thereby it tends to diminish the volume of commercial bills coming into existence and hence to turn the exchanges in our favour.

This statement is also subject to an exception. If the dear money is due to widespread optimism, belief in the continuance of an existing boom and of a state of rising prices, then dear money may fail to deter buyers. Such was the case from about November, 1919, to April, 1920.

Having investigated the effect on exchange rates of variations on the market rate of discount, we are in a position to examine the manner in which another one of the interest rates, namely, Bank Rate, is used as the regulator of the exchanges.

Let us take the case where the exchange is unfavourable. Owing to prolonged depression, the adverse exchange fails to stimulate the export trade and thus act as an automatic corrective, as it would otherwise do. High interest rates abroad attract our gold, and the exchanges continue to go against us. The New York rate, let us say, is approaching the point (about 4·84) at which gold will begin to leave the country. It is under such conditions that the regulating machinery of the Bank of England's rate comes into operation.

It may be asked: Why the Bank of England more than any other bank? Supposing gold was sent abroad by bullion dealers, in what way did that directly affect the Bank of England? In this way: the Bank of England keeps the only material gold reserve in the country, so that the sending of any quantity of gold out of the country means the diminution, sooner or later, of the reserve in the Bank of England's vaults. The bullion dealers may be acting for a banker, or for a foreign banker with an office in London. They will simply present notes at the Bank of England to the value of the gold they want, and the bank is bound by statute to give gold for those notes up to any amount. When, therefore, the exchange begins to approach the lower gold point, the Bank of England is forced to take an active interest in the matter.

The ultimate aim of the Bank of England is to protect its gold reserve, and this requires that the exchanges should be turned in our favour. This it aimed at accomplishing by raising the market rate of discount. The raising of that rate, once it can be accomplished, will effect the turning of adverse into favourable exchanges in the manner already explained. The Bank of England's immediate aim, then, is to raise the market rate of discount.

Its first step is to raise bank rate. The sequence of events in the money market is then, according to Mr.

Withers,[1] as follows. The next step lies with the joint-stock banks. Everybody in Lombard Street knows that the aim of the Bank of England in raising its rate is to send up interest rates generally and the market rate of discount in particular. The joint-stock banks may either follow the lead or not. If they decide to follow the lead, they are accepting as a fact that money is going to become dearer, i.e. that cash will become more valuable as against bills. Their aim will then become to increase their cash in hand, and this they will do in three ways:

(*a*) They will raise their rate of interest on deposits.

(*b*) They will for the present refrain from buying any more bills.

(*c*) They will call in their loans at call and short notice.

Their short-dated loans will have been made in the main to bill-brokers. This calling in places the the bill-brokers in a very unfortunate position. They are hit in three ways:

(1) First of all the bills they had in their portfolio become automatically less in value, since interest rates have gone up. Interest rates going up means that more discount will be deducted from the bills when the holders want to turn them into cash than was the case before. A bill is worth less in terms of cash, so that the whole portfolio of bills which the broker was carrying becomes worth less.

(2) The banks are calling in the loans on which the bill-brokers had been financing their business.

(3) The banks are not buying bills to the extent that that had been, just when the brokers want to turn them into cash.

Obviously, the bill-broker has to get financial accommodation somewhere, and, the joint-stock banks refusing to help him, the only place he can get it is at the Bank of England. The Bank of England is perfectly willing

[1] "The Meaning of Money," Chapter XII.

to let him have it, but on its own terms: approved bills it will discount at bank rate, loans it will make at a half per cent. above bank rate. That means that bank rate has become the effective market rate. People who had bills to discount have to discount them at bank rate. Bank rate determines the price for advances. Rates of interest have been raised all round; the market rate of discount has been forced up to the level of bank rate. The Bank of England has achieved its object. The raising of market rate has had the effect of turning the exchanges in our favour in the manner described above.

Now let us suppose the joint-stock banks do follow the lead of the Bank of England. The Bank of England wants to make money dearer, but the joint-stock banks do not follow its lead. They neither refrain from buying bills nor call in their short loans to the bill-brokers. The Bank of England can make them follow its lead. It can go into the money market and borrow money, which it does not need, in order to make money scarcer. Money becomes scarce as a result of the Bank's borrowings. Everybody in Lombard Street knows that, whether they like it or not, money is becoming dearer. From that point, the developments are exactly as in the previous case. The joint-stock banks have no option but to refrain from buying bills, and strengthen their cash reserves by calling in their short loans and raising deposit rates. The bill-brokers have to borrow. Once again, therefore, bank rate becomes effective, and the forces described above are set in motion and turn the exchanges in Britain's favour.

The method adopted by the Bank of England in borrowing in the circumstances named would be to borrow either from the joint-stock banks or from bill-brokers; in both cases the loan would be covered by the deposit of securities. The first alternative would reduce directly the balances which the joint-stock banks keep at the Bank of England; the second would reduce them indirectly, for the making of a loan by bill-brokers to the Bank of England would take the form of cheques drawn by the bill-brokers in question on the joint-stock banks. In both cases, therefore, the amount of the joint-stock banks' balances at the Bank of England would be reduced, and the basis on which they create credit narrowed accordingly.

The Bank Return would of course show a decrease in liabilities under the head of deposits, and a corresponding decrease in assets under the head of securities.

It is not possible to give a recent case of this procedure being followed, because since the banking amalgamations produced the Big Five, the latter have been in general agreement with the policy of progressive deflation pursued by the Treasury and the Bank of England, and have in practice always followed the Bank of England's lead; moreover, other devices have been brought into operation, not by the Bank of England but by the Government itself, to safeguard the exchange position against the dangers caused by a depreciated currency and an excessive Floating Debt: prohibition of gold exports until the spring of 1925, embargo on foreign loans, credits in New York. A striking example of the effectiveness of rises in bank rate in turning the exchanges in Britain's favour occurred in the first days of August, 1914. With the approach of war, every one in all the principal cities of the world who had claims elsewhere tried to realize them in terms of his own currency. All the financial centres of the world were trying to bring their balances home. The Bank of England raised its rate from 4 per cent. to 10 per cent, in the course of a few days, and this was so effective that the exchanges went violently in favour of this country and remittances arrived from almost every foreign centre until the means of remittance were exhausted.

Before the war bank rate was or could be made effective in regulating all British exchange rates. During the war this regulation was in suspension through the pegging of the only rate that mattered—the New York rate.[1] From 1918 up to the return to the gold standard in 1925 bank rate was unable to perform its function with any appreciable effect, since the war had destroyed the two assumptions on which the reasoning of this chapter is based. The first of those assumptions is that British legal tender is convertible into gold; the second is that claims on foreign centres can be realized if gold in desired.

The necessity of these assumptions is evident. The purpose of manipulating bank rate, so far as the exchanges are concerned, is to turn them in our favour by attracting gold from abroad. Now gold would not be likely to come from abroad so long as no security existed that it could not be got back again on demand. For bank rate to be effective as a regulator of the exchanges a free gold market is therefore necessary, and also elsewhere, for high interest rates here cannot attract gold if foreign governments refuse to allow it to come.

Before the war both the assumptions in question held good, the first regarding the convertibility of British currency invariably, the second regarding the possibility of getting gold from foreign centres usually, though not quite invariably.

From 1918 to 1925, the first assumption did not hold good, and the second was valid only as regards New York. In 1925, the convertibility of British currency into gold was restored, so that the first assumption is again valid; and the restoration of the convertibility of the currencies of Sweden, Holland, the Union of South Africa, Australia and New Zealand has restored the validity of the second assumption so far as those countries, and the United States, are concerned.[2] In regard to other countries than those named, the second assumption is still invalid

[1] See Chapter IX.

[2] The upper and lower gold points, London on New York, are respectively 4·90606 and 4·84103. Firms possessing special facilities find it worth while shipping before these theoretical points are reached.

and outside them, therefore, the machinery will not work.[1]

Since the return to gold, rises in bank rate, which operate on the free gold markets mentioned above, have again been effective, as in December, 1925, in influencing the exchanges in Britain's favour. It has to be observed, however, that there exists to-day, as a result of the war, a weakness in London's position as against New York in respect of the greater resources and gold reserves of the latter centre,[2] as a result of which manipulations of bank rate against the monetary policy of New York would probably be of little effect. Before the war the relation between the two was exactly opposite, as the events of July–August, 1914, showed.

[1] And, of course, is not required to.
[2] See Chapter XVIII.

CHAPTER XII

INFLATION

WE now come to the last and most interesting section of the whole subject—to the consideration, namely, of the sixth factor which causes exchange fluctuations, i.e. the depreciation of currency by the issue of paper money. Of all the disastrous effects of the war on finance and the foreign exchanges, that of the over-issue of paper money is the most fundamental. This over-issue is bound up with what is known as "inflation," and it is necessary to be clear as to what is meant by that term. There are two things which may be inflated, credit and currency. Inflation of currency means an increase in the volume of currency without an equivalent increase in its gold backing or in the volume of other commodities represented by it. Inflation of credit means an increase in the volume of credit without any equivalent increase in either the gold basis or in the volume of commodities available. The relations between the inflation of currency and the inflation of credit have been the subject of a great deal of technical discussion by specialists. In actual fact, the two have always during and since the war appeared together, like the high temperature and the congestion of the lungs in Spanish influenza; and the effect of the combination has been the depreciation of the currencies affected, i.e. their diminution in value in terms of gold and in terms of other currencies not so affected.

On the whole it seems best to regard the inflation of currency as the effect of the inflation of credit, the latter coming first in the order of cause and effect. Our problem is, then, twofold: (*a*) How did the inflation of credit arise, and how did that necessitate an inflation of currency? and (*b*) Given an inflation of currency, how does that depreciate the currency?

The inflation of credit we have described as the increase in the volume of credit, i.e. purchasing power, in existence without a corresponding increase in the volume of commodities on which the credi is based. The inflation of credit was in the first instance one of the methods of financing the war, which was adopted in this and other countries. In a number of countries other thatn Britain, itwas continued after the war had ended to finance current expenditure.

There are three ways, and three ways only, in which a war can be financed: taxation, borrowing, and inflation.[1] Taxation consists in the taking of purchasing power by the Government from private individuals. As a result of taxation the purchasing power of the individual is restricted to exactly the same extent as the purchasing power of the Government is increased. For every 5s. which the Government takes from us in income tax, we have 5s. less to spend. There is no inflation there, as there is no increase in the purchasing power. The second method of financing a war is borrowing: borrowing money which has been saved. When some of our more fortunate citizens, whose duties confined them to the home front during the war, subscribed for War Loan out of their savings, they diminished their potential purchasing power by exactly the same extent as that by which the Government's purchasing power was increased by the transfer of the money for War Loan to the Government's credit. There is no inflation there, because once again there is no increase in purchasing power. The fact that there is no inflation in either of these cases does not of course mean that they are without injurious effect on the national welfare. In so far as the money taken from the taxpayer, or subscribed by the applicant for War Loan, would have been spent on personal luxury, no harm is done. The wealth is wasted, alike whether it is spent on munitions or in luxurious living.

[1] See Withers: "War-Time Financial Problems," Chapter III.

But it might have been spent in a manner which would have ultimately increased the production of wealth. If, for example, instead of investing £100 in War Loan, "A" had invested it in a cotton mill, the result of his expenditure would have been ultimately to increase the production of yarn or of piece-goods. As it was, the £100 he subscribed to War Loan was spent by the Government in munitions, which were destroyed without producing any wealth. To the extent to which the money confiscated by taxation or subscribed to loans would otherwise have been applied to wealth production, to that extent such war finance is harmful. Our point here, however, is simply that in these cases there is no immediate increase in purchasing power relative to commodities, and consequently no immediate rise in prices.

The third method of financing the war, by inflation itself, is also operated by borrowing on the part of the Government, but by borrowing of a different kind. Inflation of credit in this country has taken place through the borrowing by the Government of purchasing power which did not exist. This apparently fantastic procedure took two different forms. The forms were different according as the Government borrowed the purchasing power which did not exist from the joint-stock banks, or from the Bank of England.[1]

(*a*) *Borrowing from the Joint-Stock Banks.*—Considerable pressure was put by the Government on the banks to induce them to subscribe for War Loan and to create credits which should be used to facilitate subscriptions from the banks' clients for War Loan. The banks accordingly drew on their balances at the Bank of England either to subscribe themselves for War Loan, or to create in their books credits out of which they could render to their clients the necessary overdrafts to enable those clients to sub-

[1] See, on the three following paragraphs, Mr. McKenna's speech at the annual meeting of the London Joint City and Midland Bank in 1920, reported in the weekly Press under date, January 31, 1920.

scribe. Government securities were issued to the banks and their clients, in exchange for which the Government received the purchasing power represented by the banks' former balances with the Bank of England. So far there was no inflation, because the increased spending power which the Government now had was compensated for by the decrease in the banks' balances at the Bank of England. The Government used the spending power thus put into its hands to pay contractors. The contractors paid in the drafts they received from the Government Departments to their own banking accounts. That increased the general volume of deposits which the joint-stock banks held. Out of that increased volume of deposits the joint-stock banks were able to replenish their balances at the Bank of England, which had been depleted in the first instance. The position then was that the banks' balances at the Bank of England were as they were before: the contractors' balances at their own banks were larger than they were before by exactly the amount of the increased spending power which had been created. In other words, the amount of credit available, that is, the amount of purchasing power available, had been increased by the extent to which the War Loan had been paid for out of credit created for the purpose, such credit created for the purpose being represented among the banks and their clients by Government securities. There had been an increase in the total volume of purchasing power, against which there was no increase whatever in the total volume of commodities in existence. That, in the terms of our definition, constitutes inflation. This was the first way in which inflation occurred.

(*b*) *Borrowing from the Bank of England.*—The second way was worse. It consisted of borrowing by the Government from the Bank of England on Ways and Means advances. The procedure in this case was that the Bank of England, instead of the joint-stock banks, created an overdraft in favour of the Government, which drew on it to pay contractors. The contractors paid the drafts into their accounts at the banks, which as before increased the total volume of banking deposits. This enabled the joint-stock banks to increase their balances at the Bank of England. The difference from the previous method consisted in this: that in the second case the joint-stock banks' balances had not been depleted at the commencement of the operation.

In this case, therefore, at the conclusion of the whole operation the position was that there had been an increase (*i*) in the total volume of the joint-stock banks' balances at the Bank of England, and (*ii*) in the total volume of bank deposits. Now the joint-stock banks' balances at the Bank of England constitute the funds on the basis of which the joint-stock banks found their advances to customers. Therefore, when their balances with the Bank of England were increased, the banks were in a position to make more advances than they had made before, so that in this case the inflation which finally resulted from the borrowing by the Government from the Bank of England was two-fold. There was an increase in the volume of banking deposits to the credit of the general public, and secondly there was an increase in the credit facilities which the joint-stock banks were able to grant. In other words, the dose of inflation under this second procedure was a double one, and not as in the first case a single dose. In both cases the result was to create an increase in the total volume of purchasing power available with no corresponding increase in the production of commodities.

We are now able to understand why the inflation of credit, as described above, brought in its trail an inflation of the currency. Many of the cheques which the contractors drew on their balances with the banks had to be paid in the form of £1 notes, because the money was required for paying wages. The banks therefore required an additional stock of Bradburys. They got them by drawing on their balances at the Bank of England. A certain amount, corresponding of course to the quantity of Bradburys they required, was transferred in the books of the Bank of England from the credit of the bank in question to the credit of the currency note account, and the Bradburys were then issued to the banks. Such was the actual procedure whereby the currency note was put into circulation. The issue of paper money is seen to be an adjunct to the inflation of credit, but an indispensable adjunct in the sense that only by that means could the additional purchasing power created be made effective. The volume of currency had been increased without any corresponding increase in the volume of commodities. But it is well to remember that, as Mr. McKenna has put it, "currency notes are not so much the effective cause of the rise in prices, but rather the rain-gauge that measures the quantity of rain." The whole of this question of inflation of credit and inflation of currency can best be studied in detail in two documents. The first is the Cunliffe Committee Report issued in 1919, and obtainable at H.M. Stationery Office, and the second is the report of Mr. McKenna's speech at the annual meeting of the London Joint City and Midland Bank in 1920.[1]

Having seen how war finance brought about the inflation of credit, and how that in turn caused inflation of currency, we proceed to the second of the two questions we asked at the beginning of this chapter: the effect of the inflation of the currency on the exchanges.

That effect is merely part of the general effect of the inflation of the currency on its value. The value of a currency can be expressed in two ways: in prices, which represent its exchange value at home; and in exchange

[1] There is also a useful article in the "Times Trade Supplement" of May 28, 1921, by Frank Morrison, headed "Inflation," and a detailed study of the whole subject in Prof. Pigou's "The Political Economy of War."

rates, which represent its value abroad. The general effect of the inflation of the currency was to bring about a decline in its value. That decline was expressed in (*a*) a rise in prices, i.e. the necessity to give more currency in exchange for given commodities; and (*b*) a decline in its foreign exchange value in terms of the dollar, i.e. a decline in the number of dollars which had to be given up for one pound. The reason why many foreign exchange rates other than the dollar rate did not show the same features is that other foreign currencies were subject to the same influences as our own, many of them to a much greater degree.

The relation between the volume of currency and its value is given by what is known as the "Quantity Theory of Money." The quantity theory of money is in effect this: given that at a certain time there exists a certain volume of commodities and a certain volume of money, there will be an equation between the two representing the number of units of money that have to be given for a certain unit of commodity value. If, while the volume of commodities remains unchanged, the volume of money increases, then the number of units of money that will have to be given in exchange for the same unit of commodity value will also increase. That is the quantity theory of money. As expressed, it would be accepted as correct by economists generally. Criticisms are sometimes directed against the theory, but on examination it will be found that they do not affect the theory as stated above. One line of criticism, for example, depends upon the meaning of the word "money." Money, in the sense we are using it,[1] is not the same as currency: we take money in the general sense of purchasing power. Another line of criticism can be directed against the quantity theory of money if it is stated in the form set out some time ago in a financial journal: "If with a given quantity of money and a given

[1] See Chapter I.

quantity of goods the price of the latter be 100, then with an increase of 50 per cent. in the quantity of money, the price of the goods will be advanced in a like ratio, or if the operation be reversed, the percentage will fall in a like ratio." It is by no means certain that where there is an increase in the volume of money and no equivalent increase in the volume of goods, prices will rise in the same ratio. The ratio between the increase in prices and the increase in the volume of currency depends upon the way in which inflation has occurred and on the velocity of circulation of the currency, i.e. the rate at which currency units pass from hand to hand. What is certain is that an increase in the volume of currency causes an increase in the general price level. The number of units of currency which have to be given up in exchange for a given block of commodities increases, i.e. the value of the currency unit declines. The increase in the supply of these units has brought about a decline in their value. This decline in value will be expressed, not only in terms of commodity prices, but also in terms of foreign exchange rates unless, the same causes which have caused a decline in the value of the currency here have been operative at the same time elsewhere to the same or to a greater extent.

Such was the process according to the quantity theory of money, which is not merely a theory but a description of what actually happened in this and other countries during the war, and in other countries since. It can be, and has been, proved dozens of times by various sets of figures.

(1) In the spring of 1920, the Belgian Minister of Finance, in reviewing the financial position of that country, remarked on the fact that although (he was comparing the Belgian trade balances of January and February) in January, Belgian exports only just balanced their imports, while in February exports were 65 million francs as against 44 million francs in January, still the exchange had

continued to go against Belgium. From that he drew the conclusion that the country's exchange position was not entirely dependent upon its balance of trade. The explanation why a favourable trade balance had been accompanied by a decline in the rate of exchange was that during this period Belgium had continued to increase her uncovered note circulation.

(2) An official publication of the British Government, Command Paper 434 of 1920, Table 3, compared the expansion of the eleven principal countries' currencies at that time with their rates of exchange on London. The table shows that the average expansion of the currencies as compared to the United Kingdom, which is taken as 100, was 133·5, while the average rate of exchange per cent. of parity of those countries on London was 134·1. In other words, the decline in those countries' rates of exchange practically coincided with the expansion of their paper currency.[1] Similarly, statistics relating to the note issue of the countries engaged in the war follow, very broadly speaking, the same curve as is described by price curves. It will be remembered that the great rise in prices in this country took place during the last two years of the war, and the greatest expansion of the Treasury note circulation took place also during this same period. It was in the summer of 1916 that the over-issue of paper money began to assume large proportions, and it was following that time that the rise in prices ceased to be an ordinary rise, and became a series of jumps. The same connexion between inflation and the rise in prices was observed in Germany. There is in fact a considerable parallelism between the financial history of this country and of Germany during the war. Taxation, indeed, played a much greater part in Britain than it could possibly do in Germany, by reason, in the latter case, of the limited

[1] The point was made by Mr. H. H. O'Farrell in the "Sunday Times" of April 6, 1920.

powers of the Federal Government in regard to direct taxation, the falling-off of indirect taxation owing to the blockade, and the smaller volume of accumulated liquid resources. But in both cases there was the supersession of the customary foreign exchange operations by credits arranged, in the case of Germany, with the European neutrals. In both cases, moreover, the great volume of war-time inflation occurred after the close of 1916. In 1918–1919 the German Revolution and the Peace conditions differentiated the two processes by creating political conditions which rendered possible the stopping of inflation in this country while partly favouring and partly necessitating its continuance in Germany.

It is clear that inflation of credit, accompanied by the increase of inconvertible paper currency, leads to a depreciation of exchange values in terms of currencies not subject to the same degree of inflation.

We have next to examine how far the decline in a currency's exchange value, due to inflation, is likely to go.

CHAPTER XIII

PURCHASING POWER PARITY

IT will have been observed that in speaking of the depreciation of the exchanges due to inflation we have been careful to speak of the increase of "inconvertible" paper currency. In dealing with the effects on the exchanges of an increase in the volume of currency it is necessary to distinguish between an increase due on the one hand to putting into circulation additional gold or paper convertible into gold, and an increase due on the other hand to the issue of inconvertible paper. It is true that in both cases the quantity theory applies and prices rise. But in the first case the exchanges are not necessarily affected, while in the second they are. This distinction and the reason for it are vital to the elucidation of the problem how far a decline in exchange values due to inflation is likely to go.

From 1896 to 1914 the volume of gold in existence was increased by reason of the exploitation of the Rand Mines, and owing to that increase in the volume of gold, and of the credit based on it, prices rose steadily during this period. But the exchange value of our currency did not decline. The war-time increases in the volume of currency, on the other hand, consisted of inconvertible paper: and not only did prices rise, but exchange values declined.

It is true that Treasury notes were theoretically convertible into gold. But not only were difficulties put in the way of people who wanted gold for notes, but the export of gold was prohibited as a punishable offence. People were in fact sent to prison for doing what was a normal part of a bullion dealer's business before the war. If therefore the holder of a Treasury note succeeded in getting a sovereign for his Bradbury he could do nothing with it. The convertibility of the note was in fact destroyed.

The difference between an increase of paper convertible into gold and an increase of inconvertible paper is not merely one of degree. It is true that in the case of gold, or of a paper currency freely convertible into gold, a sudden increase in the volume of currency cannot obtain, as it is not possible to increase suddenly the volume of gold available for circulation. This fact ensures the relative stability of a currency freely convertible into gold, as were the currencies of the principal European countries previous to the war. In so far, however, during the pre-war period, as the volume of gold in circulation and of the credit based upon it increased more rapidly than the volume of commodities, prices rose, but without any corresponding decline in exchange values.

The essential difference between the two ways of increasing the volume of currency lies in this, that when gold is an international currency, as it was in pre-war days,[1] and the increase in the volume of currency takes the form of putting additional gold into circulation, the increase in prices will be world-wide. A portion of the additional gold will be drawn away to other countries and will affect their currencies in terms of commodity values to an equal extent, so that the exchange values of the various currencies will remain the same. From 1896 to 1914 the gold point theory was in operation: gold could be, and when necessary was, shipped abroad and operated to equalize the rise in prices in the various countries. This it did in two ways: (*a*) The mere fact of the import of gold tended to raise prices, both by directly increasing the volume of potential circulating media and by enabling credit to be created on that basis, while the export of it exerted the opposite effect in tending to reduce prices in the country of export. (*b*) Because gold was itself a commodity, an export

[1] See Chapter III.

from the country with the higher price level and an import to the country with the lower price level, the fact of its shipment *pro tanto* altered the balance of indebtedness in favour of the exporting country, and thus tended to turn the exchanges in its favour. In this way it happened that although in England from 1896 to 1914 the value of money in terms of goods went down, yet the exchange value of our money did not go down, because the value of other countries' money in terms of their goods was going down in about the same ratio as ours. The equation between the pound on one hand, and the franc, mark, and dollar on the other, remained the same. The value of these units in terms of gold remained constant. The whole process furnished an instructive example of the way in which gold served as an international currency.[1]

In the case of an increase in the volume of inconvertible paper currency, no such general effect is produced. Prices are raised only in the country which issues the additional paper. Inconvertible paper currency has no intrinsic value. Its value is its value as a token—what the people of a country have agreed to accept it as being worth. Its foreign exchange value depends upon its purchasing power in the country of origin ; as this declines, so does its exchange value. That value cannot be restored by shipping gold abroad, for such shipments are prohibited. The extent to which the decline will go is a matter which would appear not to be susceptible of exact generalisation. During the war, the exchanges were kept in a state of suspended animation. Since the war, the principal example of a depreciated currency, the mark, has been rendered invalid for the purposes of this reasoning by the fact that its movements have been mainly dependent on political factors and on reparation payments. In the case of every currency, many factors other than inflation have been at

[1] See T. E. Gregory: "The Foreign Exchanges Before, During and After the War."

work on the exchanges, just as they have on prices. But it seems safe to say that inflation will depreciate the exchange value of a currency to at least the extent to which it raises prices.[1] Its influence on exchange value may be greater than on prices, since the element of apprehension of discounting an unfavourable future plays a larger part in exchange transactions conducted with or between foreigners than it does in determining commodity prices at home. The exchange value, in other words, will depend not only on its actual purchasing power but on its potential purchasing power, that is to say, the purchasing power which exchange dealers believe it will have in the near future. Its value is the measure of the goods that it is expected to be able to buy. Where a country is not producing any goods, as in Russia in 1919–1920, or where people have entirely lost confidence in its ability to purchase anything in the near future, as in Germany in the summer of 1923, the value goes down to nil. The activities of speculators in the currencies of the various European countries simply amount to the discounting beforehand of the probabilities in regard to the purchasing power of the paper currencies. The continued increase of paper money thus produces on exchange rates certainly the same effects as it does on home prices; and may have another, secondary, effect in lowering the credit of the issuing country.

The first statement generalizes what occurred, as a result of the war and of the events which followed it, to the currencies of the European countries as compared with that of the United States. Its truth is best illustrated by measuring the depreciation of the gold sovereign in terms of the paper pound during the period 1919–1925, which will be found to be also the measure of the depreciation at that time of the Anglo-American Exchange. Before the war the price of gold was fixed, as the Mint would always buy it at 85s. per oz. of fine gold. English standard gold

[1] See "Monetary Reform," by Prof. J. M. Keynes.

was $\frac{11}{12}$th fine, and was therefore accordingly bought at 77s. 10½d. per oz. On a given day in 1922 the price of gold was 95s. per oz. The price therefore of one ounce of standard gold, i.e. of 480 grains, was $\frac{11}{12} \times 95$. In a gold sovereign there are 123·2 grains of gold. Therefore the price of the gold in a gold sovereign in terms of the then paper pound was :

$$\frac{11 \times 95 \times 123{\cdot}2}{12 \times 480} = 22{\cdot}37\text{s.},$$

i.e. the paper pound had depreciated 2·37s. on every 22·37s. or nearly 10·6 per cent. On the same day the dollar was quoted at 4·36, i.e. a depreciation, when comparison is made with par value, of ·51 for every 4·87, or nearly 10·5 per cent. Similarly on a day when the dollar rate was 3·88, the price of fine gold was £5 6s. 8d. per oz., so that the depreciation at that time was in each case about 20 per cent.

A comparison [1] again, of the prices in Italian paper lire of (*a*) the pound sterling and (*b*) 100 gold lire, made in March, 1920, when the pound sterling was relatively stable, showed that the two sets of prices were following the same curve. The figures showed that the depreciation of the paper lire, measured in terms of (*a*) the gold lire and of (*b*) the stable pound sterling, was roughly the same in both cases.

It is inflation which was the case of the chaotic condition of the European exchanges during the half decade following the war. This country, although it changed its currency from gold to one of inconvertible paper, nevertheless over-issued paper money less than any other gold-currency country in the world except the United States, Sweden and Holland. The result is that on the one hand this country's currency in terms of the dollar declined in value,

[1] The Tables are given in the " Anglo-Italian Review " of March, 1920.

and on the other hand that in terms of other countries' currencies it appreciated, not because it itself increased its intrinsic value, but because the other countries over-issued paper money to a greater extent. The League of Nations published some very interesting economic memoranda in 1920, showing that at that time the principal countries of the world, exclusive of Russia, had increased their note-circulation eight times over. After that date the process went much further. These facts convey an idea of the extent to which inconvertible paper money had taken the place of gold as the basis of the principal currencies of the world.

The element of theoretical reasoning which surrounds the exact relations between inflation, the exchanges, and prices must not be allowed to obscure the fact, which is as well established as anything in economics can be, that inflation causes enormous rises in prices and declines in exchange values.

It follows that the exchange fluctuations of inflated currencies present quite a different problem from those of pre-war days. They can no longer be correlated to Mint Par, which assumes convertibility into gold. Our post-war experience is so varied that it is difficult to generalize from it. It seems that the present-day exchanges tend[1] to move about a new par called "Purchasing Power Parity."[2] The old Mint Par was obtained by comparing the amounts of gold which two standard coins represented. The new purchasing power parity is obtained by comparing prices in the two countries in question. We find that in the autumn of 1922 a certain block of commodities could, after making certain allowances, be purchased in England for so many pounds and in Germany for so many paper marks. The division of that number of paper marks by the corresponding number of pounds gives as quotient a figure which represents the

[1] In the absence of governmental regulations.

[2] The following explanation of purchasing power parity is based on the treatise by Prof. J. M. Keynes previously cited.

number of paper marks which a pound is worth in terms of purchasing power. Purchasing power parity, in other words, gives the exchange value of one currency in terms of another by means of an equation based on the prices obtaining in the two countries in question for certain kinds of goods. Mint Par was a comparison of quantities of gold; purchasing power parity is a comparison of certain kinds of commodity prices.

So far everything is straightforward enough; the difficulties occur in determining the two price levels to be compared. It will have been observed that in describing these price levels we made use of two qualifications. The price levels in question (*a*) were those of "certain kinds of goods"; and (*b*) these prices were to be compared "after making certain allowances."

As regards (*a*), the price levels compared are not the general price levels of the two countries, but the price levels in those countries of the goods entering into international trade. Goods and services produced at home for domestic consumption do not in either case enter into the calculation. The prices of, e.g., houses are excluded; so also are rail freights. The reason for this qualification is that a person, e.g. outside Germany, holding paper marks can only exercise the purchasing power of his paper marks on goods which it is legally and practically possible to import from Germany, i.e. on some portion of the goods entering into international trade.

As regards (*b*), in calculating the price level of the goods entering into international trade, allowance has to be made for freights, customs duties, and import and export prohibitions and regulations, for whether such prohibitions and regulations are made by governments or by organizations of producers or sellers, they may create artificial differences between home and export prices.

The price levels from the comparison of which the purchasing power parity between two countries is obtained are thus differentiated from the general price levels obtaining in those countries, (*a*) by being restricted to the goods entering into international trade, and (*b*) by being subject to the adjustment described above. The equation between the two price levels so determined gives a new parity, round about which actual rates will fluctuate, as in pre-war days they fluctuated round Mint Par.

Why must this new equilibrium be established? Why must the exchange values of a currency approximate, sooner or later, to purchasing power parity?

Suppose exchange values are lower—e.g. suppose the Berlin exchange rate to be paper Mk. 2,200 = £1 and the purchasing power parity to be paper Mk. 2,000 = £1. The latter equation means that the price of a certain quantity of goods, after making the necessary allowances for freights and duties, etc., is £1 or paper Mk. 2,000. Now the cost of paper Mk. 2,000 is $£\frac{2,000}{2,200} = 18{\cdot}182$ shillings. The holder of sterling, accordingly, can by expending 18·182 shillings buy paper Mk. 2,000, which will purchase a quantity of goods which he can sell for £1, thereby making an exchange profit—in addition to whatever trading profit he may make—of 1·812 shillings on every pound. In such circumstances a demand will be set up for paper marks, and this demand, providing no other factors intervene, will send up their value. The demand will continue so long as the exchange value is less than purchasing power parity. On the other hand, suppose the exchange value of the currency to be higher than its purchasing power parity. In that case holders of the currency will exchange it for other currencies which command greater quantities of goods than do their own; and this selling will diminish exchange value. The reasoning is the same as in the previous case applied in the reverse direction. The selling pressure will continue until the exchange value of the currency in question has declined to a point where the amount of the foreign currency exchanged for it will purchase only the same quantity of goods as are purchasable by itself, i.e. until purchasing power parity is reached.

This reasoning will incidentally have illustrated why, in calculating purchasing power parity, it is necessary to take the price levels of the goods entering into international trade, and to make the allowances set out under (*b*) above.

It will further be noted that these processes are what will take place provided no other factors intervene. It may happen on occasion that the exchange rate between two countries, as actually quoted, does not in fact approximate to purchasing power parity. In that case it is certain that there will be alterations in either the price levels in question—in one or both—or in the exchange rate, or in both; and that as a result purchasing power parity and the exchange rate will approximately coincide. It may be that at the minute the exchange value of one of the currencies is depressed by political apprehensions; these turn out to be ill-founded, and exchange values will then rise, for the reasons described above, until rates correspond with purchasing power parity. In this case it has been the exchange rate which has adjusted itself to the price level. On the other hand, political events, reparations payments or war-debt repayments may cause the exchange value of the currency affected permanently to decline. Once again there will be a gap between exchange rates and purchasing power parity. On this occasion the tendency for the exchange rate to improve in the manner described above is overborne by the effect of the blow dealt at the country's credit, wealth, or productive capacity. As therefore the decline in exchange values is permanent, imports will cost more and prices rise. The prices of the goods entering into international trade will rise until they reach the cost of replacement under the new conditions, i.e. until they reach world-prices. In this way a new purchasing power parity is reached which corresponds with exchange rates. In this sequence of events, which has happened more than once since the war in Germany, it is the price level which has adjusted itself to the exchange rate. Finally, it is conceivable that at a given moment the exchange rate, having suffered a permanent decline by reason of political events, might be temporarily depressed still further by apprehension which ultimately turns out to be ill-founded, while the price level had not yet felt the full force of the permanent decline. In this event the price level would still be rising while the exchange rate was recovering. The exchange rate and purchasing power parity would then be moving towards one another. This process would continue, for the reasons described above, until they approximately coincided. In this case both the price level and the exchange rate have adjusted themselves the one to the other.

Such, in very broad outline, is the doctrine of purchasing power parity. Its practical utility evidently is restricted by the necessity of limiting the price levels taken into consideration to those of the goods which enter into international trade and by the difficulty of accurately calculating the allowances which have to be made in respect of transport costs, customs duties, etc. Attempts to correlate the general price levels with exchange rates assume that the general price level in a country rises and falls in the same manner as the prices of the goods entering into international trade. This assumption may only be true, at any given moment of time, to a limited and uncertain extent, as the divergence between the internal and the external value of the mark during 1920–1922 fully illustrates, and that between the internal and the external value of the franc in 1925 and 1926.[1] To

[1] In June, 1922, when general prices in Germany were very low when translated into sterling, the price of a suit of clothes was higher than the corresponding price in England.

calculate, in any given case, how far the general price level is subject to influences which are not operative on the prices of the goods which enter into international trade is evidently an extremely difficult matter. The theory of purchasing power parity cannot accordingly be applied to the general price level as determined by, e.g., the Board of Trade Index Number of wholesale prices or the Labour Ministry's Index Number of retail prices. The practical utility of the theory is thus limited, but it nevertheless provides a useful general guide to the post-war movements of the exchanges.

Purchasing power parity, unlike mint par, is a variable figure: it varies with price levels. Before the war, price levels were limited in their movements by the same factor which limited the movements of exchange rates: the possibility of shipping gold. Prices expressed in terms of national currencies were in reality gold prices, for these currencies represented a claim to gold which could be enforced. Alterations in prices were accordingly alterations in gold prices. Such alterations were both gradual, since the supply of gold cannot suddenly be increased, and common to all gold-using countries, by reason of the possibility of shipping gold. An increase in prices in any one centre would mean the export of gold to other centres where prices were lower, i.e. where gold would purchase more: the lessening of the supply of gold in the first centre reduced the credit based on it and caused prices there to fall, while its import into the second centre caused prices to rise. The extent to which the relation of price levels to each other could alter was fixed by the Gold Points; purchasing power parity, therefore, which expresses the relation of price levels to one another, was bound to be found somewhere between the Gold points. There it still is, in the case of countries where the Gold Point hypothesis still holds good, i.e. which have a free gold market, and where there has been time for prices to adjust themselves to it.[1] To-day the possibility of shipping gold frequently does not exist. Many countries however, do not possess sufficient to ship, about half the world's available supply being already in the U.S.A. In the case of currencies which have lost their gold value, prices and hence purchasing power parities depend on a number of variable factors such as the extent of industrial and agricultural production and the quantity of paper money a government has printed and is expected to print. These purchasing power parities have accordingly been separated from the Gold Points for an indefinite period. The only questions there are, are whether the exchange rates which tend to fluctuate about these purchasing power parities can be stabilized, i.e. whether the currencies in question can be made exchangeable against gold, or against some currency like the dollar or the pound which is on an actual gold basis; this would fix the exchange rate and also therefore ultimately the purchasing power parity, and thus avoid the wide fluctuations of the years immediately following the war. Another way of achieving the same result, in theory, would be to stabilize the price level: this would anchor purchasing power parity to a fixed figure, and the exchange rate would, on the reasoning of this chapter, ultimately come to rest round about the same figure. But controlling price levels over a period of time is so difficult in practice that Governments have not attempted it since the war; and where serious efforts to stabilize currency values have been made, it has invariably been the first method, that of anchoring the exchange rate by making the currency exchangeable against gold at a fixed rate, which was adopted. This was done successfully during 1924–1925 in a number of cases of which the first and most difficult was the German Mark.

[1] On the relation between the British and U.S. price levels, see Chapter XVI.

PART IV—THE NEW EQUILIBRIUM

CHAPTER XIV

THE MARK

THE effects on the exchanges of the outbreak of the war in 1914 have already been briefly referred to ;[1] and also the war-time expedients for pegging the Anglo-American rate.[2] During the war, all the exchanges remained in a state of suspended animation by reason of the control exercised in the belligerent countries over payments abroad. No doubt the artificial equilibrium thus maintained assisted considerably in obscuring the extent to which the economic basis of European civilization was being shattered.

In 1919 the exchanges were generally decontrolled, and the course followed since the artificial equilibrium of the war-years ended has registered the effects of the war and the resulting terms of peace on the economic health of the countries concerned. Certain of the more important of the movements and their significance will be considered in the following chapters. Here it is intended to examine the course of the German mark up to the end of 1925. It is a story of enormous depreciation through inflation, followed by stabilization and the issue of a new currency under unequalled difficulties. The case of the mark is moreover worthy of especial attention by reason of the fact that before the war Germany was the greatest industrial power on the Continent and that the devaluation of the mark (*die Entwertung der Mark*) has profoundly affected the welfare of this country both directly and indirectly, bearing as it does a share of responsibility for the unemployment existing here.

[1] Chapter XI. For a full account, see Withers: "The War and Lombard Street."

[2] Chapter IX.

From about 80 after the signature of the Peace Treaty, the mark went up to 180 by December, 1919. In the spring of 1920 it declined further to about 270, recovered in the summer to about 135, and then fell away again fairly steadily to between 350 and 400 in September, 1921. The causes of this decline up to September, 1921 may be outlined as follows:

(1) The war left Germany terribly weakened. The disastrous effects of the blockade have never been fully realized outside Central and Eastern Europe. Unable to import on any large scale, the war was conducted mainly out of Germany's own resources When the Armistice and the Revolution came, Germany was drained of all kinds of goods. Food and raw materials had to be imported; also a large quantity of manufactured goods which she herself could not produce until her people had recovered a little from semi-starvation, her factories restarted and her transport repaired.

(2) The Peace Treaty took away large and rich territories, such as the Saar coalfields, the Lorraine iron and the Alsace potash deposits, as well as the corn and potato-producing lands of Posen and West Prussia. Further, large deliveries of coal had continuously to be made by Germany to France, and also to Belgium and Italy. A large number of cows had also to be surrendered to France. The result of all this was that materials which before were exported had now to be imported; food formerly produced at home had to be bought abroad.

(3) The Peace Treaty also took away the mercantile fleet, so that freights had to be paid in foreign currency.

(4) German exports were further hampered by the destruction of German trading connexions.

(5) A large army of occupation and numerous expensive Allied commissions were quartered on Germany, while she also had to compensate her own nationals whose property overseas had been seized by the Allied Powers.

(6) The revolutionary outbreaks dissipated still further Germany's slender resources. Nor were the revolutionary Governments immune from the extravagant officialdom and the subsidizing of favoured classes of the population, which has been one of the universal consequences of the war.

The cumulative effects of these factors were (*a*) to necessitate large purchases of foreign currency, and (*b*) to render the German Government unable to meet its obligations save by the printing of paper money. The more paper money was printed, the more the mark declined in value abroad and at home; the more the value declined, the more marks were required to purchase foreign currencies or home manufactures and labour, and the higher, therefore, became the Government's expenditure; whereupon more marks were printed. The mark, in the grip of the jagged teeth of the vicious circle, continued to decline, but, taken over a period, in a more or less steady fashion until the autumn of 1921. Then its movements became as follows:

1921.—November 30th - - -	940–1,050
December 1st - - -	700– 805
,, 31st - - -	768– 774
1922.—January 31st - - -	855– 864
February 28th - - -	990–1,017
March 31st - - -	1,250–1,380
April 29th - - -	1,250–1,260
May 31st - - -	1,219–1,240
June 30th - - -	1,600–1,670
August 1st - - -	2,690–3,010
,, 8th - - -	3,240–3,405
,, 14th - - -	3,540–3,780
,, 15th - - -	4,050–4,620

The causes of this catastrophic fall are not difficult

to trace. Unfortunately discussion of these economic phenomena has been obscured by political bias, which has ascribed the fall to the deliberate design of the German Government, motived by the desire either to place an artificial premium on Germany's export trade, or to create a situation in which the plea of poverty could be put forward to secure a remission of reparation payments, or by both intentions. The suggestion is sheer imbecility. Is the depreciation of the French franc to be ascribed to the deliberate intention of the French Government, motived by the desire to evade payment of the French debt to Britain? So far as the first alleged intention is concerned, we have already disclosed the fallacies of the argument,[1] and it would be childish to suppose that the fallacies were not known to the German financial authorities. If a depreciating exchange were of lasting benefit to the export trade, we and every other nation should obviously set about depreciating our own currencies as fast as possible. As regards the second intention alleged, it is hard to believe that statesmen would put any hope in so transparent a manœuvre, still more difficult to believe that on such a slender chance of success they would risk plunging their own country into a social cataclysm. For that is what a continually depreciating currency brings in its train. By annihilating alike the savings of years and the highest rises in wages, it brings discontent to the point of revolution. What rising prices mean in the way of social difficulties we experienced in this country in 1919–1920; and prices here rose slowly and steadily compared with what happened in Germany.

The idea that the depreciation of the mark was deliberately engineered by the Government is not only *a priori* too absurd to be believed by any intelligent person, but it is finally discredited by the actual historical sequence in which events occurred. There have been adequate

[1] See Chapter VIII on the Balance of Trade.

and sufficient reasons for depreciation in the economic conditions obtaining.

In detail, the causes of this catastrophic fall are as follows: First, the Indemnity Policy imposed by the allied French and British Governments. The latter imposed the payment of large sums of money by way of indemnities from Germany, and as German currency was an altogether fluctuating quantity, and as most other European currencies were in a like condition, it was decided that Germany must pay the indemnity in one of two ways, either in gold or dollars. Now, of course, Germany had not the gold, and therefore it meant that Germany must buy dollars, and spend marks in buying them. The dollars which they bought were not used for the purpose of paying for imports into Germany, which would be manufactured up and sent out again, but were simply handed over to the Governments of France and England. That meant that on the foreign exchange market there was suddenly a huge influx of marks. The result was what is always the result when the supply of one commodity is suddenly increased in terms of another: the value of the mark went down.

The second cause is to be found in the decision of the Allies, promulgated in the autumn of 1921, to give a large portion of Upper Silesia to Poland. In the Germany of 1914 there were three great coalfields: the Saar Valley, the Ruhr Valley, and the Upper Silesian coalfield. Of these three, the Saar Valley had been previously transferred to France, the Ruhr Valley was partly occupied in providing large quantities of coal to France at a price far below the world-market price. The third was now handed over to Poland, together with a large portion of the industrial area of Upper Silesia. We have seen that the value of a country's currency to-day is based on what the country produces, or on its ability to produce at all. Taking away Upper Silesia reduced Germany's ability to produce, consequently the mark fell at once. The date on which the mark began its catastrophic fall in the autumn of 1921 coincided exactly with the date on which the news was received in Berlin that the decision in regard to Upper Silesia was going to be enforced.

The December, 1921, recovery of the mark was apparently due to hopes raised by the Washington Conference and by rumours of a credit to Germany to be arranged in London. The catastrophic fall from March, 1922, up to the end of that year was due to: (*a*) further far-reaching demands made by the Reparations Commission which involved foreign control over Germany's finances, control comparable to the kind formerly exercised in Turkey; (*b*) the failure, owing to French opposition, of the negotiations for a loan; (*c*) the standing likelihood of French aggression against Germany's only remaining coalfield, the Ruhr Valley, expressed by M. Poincaré in his Sunday speeches throughout the second half of 1922; (*d*) as a result of the continually rising prices, the instability of German political and social life. These conditions lowered German credit still further and deprived public opinion of any confidence in the financial future of the country. The indemnity policy and the taking away of mineral and agricultural land had a continuous and cumulative effect; the economic position of Germany became increasingly unsound and the mark increasingly weak. It is worthy of note that, as Mr. Keynes has pointed out, on occasion the increase in the note circulation was not the cause but the effect of the decline in value of the mark. The order of causation frequently was that political causes sent down the value of the mark; the consequent rises in wages and prices increased the German Government's expenses and rendered it unable to meet its short-term obligations (Treasury bills) as they matured; hence it printed notes to meet the deficit.

Why, it may be asked, did not the activity of German

workshops in 1920–1922 redress the balance? Because the German "boom" was far more illusory than the English boom of 1920. Germany's trade balance remained unfavourable. She imported more than she exported. So many mineral and other resources had been taken away from her, the quantity of food and raw materials required to be imported was still so great,[1] that her trade balance still showed a deficit, and this in spite of the limitation of consumption enforced on the mass of the German people. The confiscation of German shipping and overseas investments meant that there were no appreciable "invisible exports" to offset this deficit, as is the case in England and was the case in Germany prior to the war. Germany, that is, in spite of her industrial activity, was not paying her way—altogether apart from reparations payments.

The indemnity, however, can ultimately be paid only in goods. If it is insisted that Germany pays in gold or in dollars, she can only obtain them by selling goods to other countries. The payment of an indemnity implies, even apart from the devaluation of the mark, a surplus of exports, i.e. a big export trade. This, in turn, in a world whose buying power is diminished, implies unemployment elsewhere. But as, in spite of Germany's industrial activity, her exports did not provide a surplus over her imports, it followed that to buy the dollars insisted upon it was necessary to print notes to pay for them, and thus continually to diminish the value of the mark. The resulting artificial cheapening of German export prices provided an example of the limited benefit of a depreciating exchange.[2] If an English price in pounds and a German price in marks, quoted on Tuesday to a Dutch buyer, work out the same in florins, and on Thursday he finds he can get one-third more marks for his florins than

[1] The coal deliveries insisted on by France were so large that Germany, previously a coal-exporting country, had now, after losing the Saar and Silesian coalfields, to import coal and pay for it in foreign currency.

[2] See Chapter VIII.

he could on Tuesday, his price has been reduced by 33 per cent., and in that cause of course the quality of the article being equal, he buys the German goods. The price in German marks is the same, but the price to him has gone down. A market is thereby provided for German goods to the exclusion of others. At the same time the devaluation of the mark made imports into Germany dearer, and thereby made still more impossible the bridging of the gulf between imports and exports. German prices were always approximating upwards to world-prices, and sometimes reached them, as was the case, e.g. early in 1922, in the paper trade. But then some political cause caused the mark to depreciate and set the whole process in motion again. The Germany economy was gripped by the jagged teeth of the vicious circle.

A great deal of German capital was lost during this period through selling below cost, for it became impossible to calculate costs when prices and wages were constantly altering. Some exporters who sold in stable foreign currency—dollars or sterling—and simply based their prices on world market prices, were able to preserve their liquid capital; but many were unable to do so and lost their working capital. German manufacturers working for the home trade got into a hopeless position, for they never knew what their costs would be by the time their goods were completed, and still less what the mark prices at which they had sold would be worth in terms of goods or foreign currency when the accounts were collected.

The chaotic state of German trade reacted to the disadvantage of this country, apart from creating the competition of artificially cheap exports, in the following way. Germany was before the war not only Britain's second largest customer, but also a large customer of many countries which in turn bought from Britain. A Chilean nitrate exporter, a Brazilian coffee exporter, would employ the funds received from their sales to Hamburg in purchasing piece goods from Manchester. The devaluation of the mark destroyed German purchasing power, and German imports had to be restricted to food and essential raw materials. She could buy neither from us. Our own overseas customers, who could no longer sell to Germany, were no longer able to buy from us.

The volume of cheap exports which Germany sent out rested on the economic basis of low wages. The devaluation of the mark proceeded alike in terms of foreign currencies and in terms of commodities, though not to the same extent. Prices rose to an enormous extent, wages and salaries to nothing like that extent. Real wages were far below what they were before the war: salaries, in terms of what they would buy, were at starvation rates. In June, 1922, prices had risen in the case of foodstuffs between 60 and 70 times the pre-war figures; in the case of clothing between 80 and 100 times. Wages had risen on an average about 25 times; the middle grade of salaries between 7 and 11 times; fixed incomes, of course, not at all.[1] The result is that wage-earners had a lower standard of life than before the war and the middle classes a very much lower standard. The wage-earners became thoroughly discontented, because they had continually increasing wages which meant nothing, on account of the increased prices. Neither they nor still less salaried classes could keep up with the increased cost of living. The purchasing power of the other section of the middle classes (those who live on fixed incomes) had long since disappeared. Every further step in the devaluation of the mark made German

[1] The above figures are quoted from an article by Mr. H. N. Brailsford in the "Nation" of July 15, 1922. They were originally given by the Prussian Premier to the Landtag, and their accuracy is, in Mr. Brailsford's experienced judgment, established by his own investigations. The present writer, who was himself in Germany at that time, is able to confirm them from his own investigation.

A bank clerk was then earning, in terms of what money would buy, roughly the equivalent of £1 per week; medium grade civil servants and commercial employees such as secretaries and accountants roughly one-quarter of the real remuneration they would receive in Britain.

exports cheaper, widened the gulf between imports and exports, confiscated savings and reduced the real value of wages and salaries. The result was that with the rising prices the home purchasing power ultimately collapsed.

In all this there is nothing surprising. A considerable part of what happened in regard to the mark exchange was prophesied by Professor Keynes in 1919.[1] Nor, even at that time, was he alone in his prophecy.

Whether the policy pursued by the peoples victorious in the Great War was, on purely political grounds, a desirable one is not here in question. The subject of foreign exchange must deal largely with international economics, and students of it are compelled to furnish explanations of the phenomena they find. In doing so they cannot avoid temporary excursions into the dangerous No Man's Land which connects Economics with Politics, without thereby trespassing over the boundaries of the latter. Whatever view be taken, on other than economic grounds, of the policy pursued towards Germany, there is no doubt that it did in fact cause the devaluation of the mark and the results therefrom above set out.

There were, of course, interests in Germany to whom inflation was advantageous—those, speaking generally, who were working on borrowed money. Agriculturalists encumbered by mortgages, industrialists burdened by loans which they had contracted in the form of overdrafts or debentures, saw their obligations automatically wiped out; for their debts were measured in paper marks which came to signify continually less in terms of the produce which they themselves sold. In some cases these people welcomed inflation; in other cases they were hit by it in other ways, so that the advantage of seeing their loan obligations wiped out was offset by, e.g., the disadvantage of losing capital through not being able to get in their paper mark accounts until the debts themselves had

[1] "The Economic Consequences of the Peace."

lost value. The interests which profited by inflation would not by themselves have been able to force the policy of inflation on Germany, and did not in fact do so. It was the burdens laid on Germany for political reasons—the occupation of the Rhineland, the deliveries of coal, the Reparations payments—which were directly and primarily responsible for the increased note-issue in Germany and for the consequent devaluation of the mark.

With the social effects of this catastrophic process—the extinguishing among large sections of the population of all opportunity for culture in the struggle to keep alive—it is impossible to deal here; but the attempts of the economic organism to adjust itself to a continually depreciating currency should be noticed. (1) Each fall in the mark was accompanied by a rise in the value of Industrial shares because these shares represented property in fixed assets such as land, buildings, etc., which would not automatically lose their value with the next fall of the mark, as will, e.g., a bank deposit. This kind of investing was known as "the flight from the mark." (2) Soaring prices led to great difficulty in financing business. The depreciating exchange so increased the cost of manufactured articles that to replace worn out or obsolete machinery, and to carry stocks, required enormous capital. This difficulty was only very partially met by increases in the capital of firms and limited companies. These increases represented merely a revaluation of assets in terms of the depreciated currency, and were not at all necessarily an indication of development work or increased prosperity. In fact, the returns obtained in many trades were absurdly small. Dividends of hundreds per cent. in paper marks frequently shrivelled down to 2 or 3 per cent. on the gold value of the capital invested in the business.

As to liquid capital, it was simply destroyed by he loss of value of the currency, and it was impossible to restore it, for every one from richest to poorest hastened to turn money into goods or industrial shares which would not lose value automatically and immediately.

The increase in the prices of manufactured goods, among other effects, caused the point to be approached where farmers would no longer find it worth while to produce a surplus above their own requirements. The finances of the State became hopeless, for taxes fixed at the old currency values would not meet the expenditure determined by the new. As a result of all these conditions, and in turn intensifying them, discontent and loss of confidence grew to an extent which imperilled the fabric of the State and of society itself.

The end came in 1923 with the French invasion of the Ruhr. The Ruhr area is a vast coalfield—the only important one not taken away from Germany by the Peace Treaty of 1919—and the most important industrial area in Germany. In the summer of 1922 Germany had tried to get a loan abroad to restore her finances, which were being wrecked by the Allies' Reparation demands and the inflationary policy forced on Germany as a result of those demands. International banking opinion had been favourable to the idea of making such a loan, but the proposal had been wrecked by French opposition. M. Poincaré made speeches indicating his intention of making war on Germany, and throughout the autumn of 1922 the mark fell away from 1,500 into the thousands. In January, 1923, France actually invaded the Ruhr. Germany, entirely disarmed by the Peace Treaty, had nothing to oppose to the tanks and aeroplanes of the French but the passive resistance of the working population, in the form of a refusal to work. The "war" in this form extended to the Rhineland, which was mainly occupied by the French. Passive resistance meant that vast numbers of workmen went on strike and were paid by the German Government for refusing to work for the French. The population of the Rhineland and Ruhr were being supported in idleness by the impoverished remainder of Germany. Under the huge financial burden thus thrown on German finances the paper mark, after being maintained by the German Government for some months at 97,000 to the pound by use of such supplies of foreign currency as it possessed, collapsed altogether into the hundred thousands, millions, and finally billions. Passive resistance had to be abandoned during the autumn of 1923, and the German Government entered on the task of creating a new currency of stable value.

The stabilization was carried out by the German authorties in particular Dr. Schacht, President of the Reichsbank, during the winter 1923–1924, without external help, and in face of the industrial and financial disorganization brought about by the French occupation.

The new currency unit is the gold mark or Reichsmark (RM), which is based on the American dollar and the value of which is 4·2 gold marks = \$1. One gold mark is worth one billion paper marks, and on this basis the German authorities were able to stabilize the paper mark at 18½ billion to the pound on the international exchanges, where rates were for a time still quoted in paper marks, not in gold marks, although the gold mark became in 1924 the only German currency for all practical purposes. Thus the international exchange value of the paper mark was 4·2 billion paper marks = \$1 (American). The number of either paper or Reichsmarks obtained for £1 now depends, therefore, on the number of dollars which £1 will purchase: with sterling valued at \$4·80 the pound was worth 20·15 billion paper marks = RM 20·15; with sterling at parity with the dollar, the pound buys 20·43 Reichsmarks.

The Rentenmark is another German currency unit which represented the transition stage between the paper mark and the Reichsmark. Its value is the same as that of the gold mark.

These measures were later followed by a temporary

agreement about Reparations and an international loan to Germany, subscribed mainly in New York and London, and the French evacuation of the Ruhr in August, 1925.

The international loan to Germany, it is to be noted, followed, not preceded, the stabilization of the mark.

The stabilization of the mark during the winter of 1923–1924 under the terrible difficulties then existing, without external help and in face of the occupation and exploitation of Germany's most valuable industrial district by a hostile foreign army, is by far the greatest financial achievement of our time. The inability of France to stabilize the franc, in spite of incomparably more favourable conditions—internal peace and external sympathy, neither of which was possessed by Germany at the close of 1923—and in spite of the assistance rendered to France in 1923 by American financiers, indicates the enormous difficulties that attend the attempt to stabilize a depreciating currency. The success finally achieved by Dr. Schacht, who was given for the purpose practically dictatorial powers, is a tribute both to Dr. Schacht and to the German people.

Following the stabilization, some provision had to be made to deal with the case of numberless people whom the inflation had robbed of all their savings—the holders of insurance policies, mortgages, Government bonds, industrial debentures, and similar securities which were not represented by concrete assets such as plant and buildings which increased in value as the mark declined. The value of these securities, which was simply their value in terms of paper marks, had become simply *nil*. Take the case of a man who twenty years before the war had taken out a life and endowment policy for Mk. 40,000, equivalent at that time to about £2,000, who had paid his premiums regularly, and whose policy fell due for payment in the autumn of 1923. He received 40,000 paper marks, equivalent not to £2,000 but to $\frac{40,000}{18,500,000,000,000}$

of £1. The policy, that is, for which for nearly thirty years he had paid the equivalent of so many pounds per annum yielded him an infinitesimal fraction of a penny. The people who had made these investments were, generally speaking, the stea iest, most patriotic, and most hard-working, and something had to be done, once the mark was stabilized, to restore some small portion which had been taken from them by the inflation—which had operated as a gigantic capital levy applicable to certain kinds of wealth only. In the summer of 1925 a law was passed which restored a small percentage of what they had lost by "valorizing" insurance policies, debentures, government securities, etc., by a varying percentage, 25 per cent. being the highest. This law (*Aufwertungsgesetz*) provided that the securities named were henceforth to be dealt with on the basis that they were worth in gold marks something up to 25 per cent. of their face value in paper marks. The holders, therefore, after receiving compensation, were in the position of having lost something over 75 per cent. of their capital through the inflation.

With the carrying through of the stabilization of the mark a new set of conditions came into existence. The first was a shortage of liquid capital, the second a widespread inability to compete in foreign markets in spite of the low real wages paid.

The shortage of liquid capital is easy to understand. Owing to the conditions obtaining during the inflation period liquid capital had as far as possible been converted into fixed capital in the form of buildings and plant, which would not automatically lose value as the mark declined. When stabilization came much of this fixed capital was found to be useless, in the sense that it was in excess of what was required to produce the goods which the German and the foreign markets were capable of absorbing. Further, a great deal of capital had simply been lost by selling goods at under cost owing to the inability to ascertain under the chaotic conditions of that time what costs really were. The loss of capital through the inflation period was similar in kind to that incurred by the Lancashire cotton industry in selling goods under cost but in Germany it affected the entire industry of the country.

When industrialists had not converted liquid capital into either fixed capital or stable foreign currency, but had left it in the form of deposits with banks and financial houses, the latter had bought foreign currency with it; the decline in the value of the paper mark automatically released the bank from its liability to the depositor, while the foreign currency which the bank had bought retained its value. When the stabilization came the industrialist had lost his money while the bank retained it in the form of a foreign balance. The net effect of the process was, therefore, the transfer of wealth from the industrialist to the bank. Summing up this aspect of the matter, one may say that inflation benefited the industrialists and agriculturists as against the banks and the middle and manual working classes, and operated in the direction of freeing industry from the control of the banks; the stabilization operated in exactly the reverse direction, and in particular operated in the direction of restoring the control of the banks over industry, and that the financial speculator benefited all through.

The shortage of liquid capital is thus easily explicable. It was accompanied by a widespread lack of confidence which rendered its amelioration by accommodation on credit equally difficult. No one knew, when the stabilization came, how his neighbour stood—or, indeed, very frequently, how his own business stood. Every bookshop was full of textbooks explaining how balance sheets made out in terms of paper marks were to be converted into gold marks, but this took time, and until it was done the inquiry agencies were helpless in regard to answering status inquiries. In these circumstances accommodation was very difficult to obtain, and in many cases could only be secured on very onerous terms—perfectly sound and reputable firms had during 1924 to pay anything up to 35 per cent. per annum. The position was gradually eased by the inflow of foreign liquid capital into Germany, principally from the U.S. and Britain, at first in the form of short-dated banking credits and later in that of long-term loans equivalent to our mortgage debentures.

The inability to compete effectively in the world's markets during the period following the stabilization was in the first instance due to the sudden loss of the artificial cheapening of German export prices by the depreciation of the paper mark. Its real causes lie deeper, as is shown by its persistence for years after the stabilization had been carried through. To analyse these causes in detail would take us too far from our subject: we may sum them up by saying that they are simply aspects of the economic dislocation brought about by the war, the impoverishment of the world at large leading it to curtail its purchases and leading various countries to manufacture for themselves what previously they had been content to import. These general causes operate to the disadvantage of Germany just as they do to the disadvantage of Britain. In Germany their operation was nullified for years by inflation; when inflation ceased, their effect was felt suddenly in full measure.

Even the home market was unable to support industry, for during the inflation period every one who had money spent it on concrete things which would not lose value; people purchased ahead both for business and for domestic consumption, in a way they would not have done had it been possible to save, and when stabilization came the home buying power was largely exhausted.

Germany, it is true, is less handicapped than Britain by the attempt to maintain a standard of living which the economic position of the country does not justify—the middle, working, and upper classes alike have a far lower standard of living there than in Britain, and, further, the gulf between sheltered and unsheltered industries is not anything like so wide in Germany as here. As against these relative advantages, however, German industry suffers under terrible handicaps which have no counterpart in Britain: the dislocation consequent on the French invasion of the Ruhr, on the foreign occupation of the Rhineland, on the Revolution, and on inflation; the effects of years of under-nourishment both during and after the war; the almost incredible efforts made during the war, when German industry stood alone against that of the rest of the world; and the burdens laid on industry by Reparations payments. In fact, to those who know at first hand what Germany has gone through in the last decade, the wonder is that she is still able to compete at all. That ordered life did not long ago disappear is due only to the hard work, the capacity, and the self-discipline of the German people.

The deflation crisis did not reach its height until more than two years after the stabilization, i.e. until early 1926. Its development, which seemed about to reach its height in the summer of 1924, was delayed by an inflow of foreign credits. This caused the development of money- and credit-difficulties to be somewhat delayed. When the acute stage was reached it was early in 1926, 2½ years after the stabilization had been effected, and it took the form of a confidence crisis as well as of a money- and unemployment-crisis. Bankruptcies became more than double the average of pre-war figures, and a large number of businesses came to be conducted under official supervision (*Geschäftsaufsicht*)—a new process designed to meet the needs of the time which has so far had no parallel in this country, whereby a business was carried on in a kind of conditional liquidation until it became clear whether it was solvent or not. All this represented a salutary but highly unpleasant clearing of the economic system of unhealthy elements which had accumulated during the inflation period. More serious were the difficulties in which the big and entirely reputable combines found themselves, especially in the iron and steel, colliery and shipbuilding industries. The parallel with England, which will not fail to be observed, comes out as strikingly in regard to unemployment, which, after being almost negligible through the inflation period, mounted early in 1926 to over two millions, i.e. to a higher figure than obtained in England during the worst period of the slump.

One might anticipate a very slow improvement as the deflation crisis works itself out were it not for the menace of Reparations. The deflation crisis could have been eased over a period by an easier credit-and-currency policy on the part of the financial authorities until the capacity of the German people for sustained and skilled production had created the necessary basis of real wealth for a stable currency, had it not been that the currency-and-credit policy of the financial authorities was in part dictated from outside with a view to extracting as much as possible of the enormous annual payments provided for under the Reparations "settlement" made in 1924 and known as the Dawes Scheme. This, and the story of the mark after the end of 1925, will be considered later in conjunction with international debts generally.[1]

[1] Chapter XVIII.

CHAPTER XV

THE FRANC

OTHER developments during the five years following the war may be more briefly referred to. As soon as the artificial equilibrium of the war-period ended, the European currencies showed a rapid decline in terms of sterling, due in the first instance to the necessity of paying for the replenishment of stocks. Despite the general postponement in 1919 of the payment of interest on war debts owed by continental nations to Britain, these currencies continued to be inflated, and consequently to depreciate, a tendency which was intensified by political instability on the Continent. The Austrian and the Hungarian krone, the Polish mark, and the Russian rouble went the same way as the German mark. The Dutch florin and the Swedish krona, on the other hand, lost value very slightly for a time and soon returned to par value and remained there. All the other European currencies showed more or less substantial depreciation, the loss in value being least in the case of the pound and the Danish and Norwegian kronen, while the Italian lira, the Czecho-Slovak krone, and the Finnish mark fairly early attained a relative measure of stability at substantially below par value. The case of the franc and the pound sterling require fuller treatment. So far as the European currencies generally are concerned the rates obtaining reflected the damage suffered during the war and the inflation and extravagance, public and private, which followed. The "neutral" countries were drawn into the current of events owing to the reaction on them of the events which had taken or were taking place in neighbouring "belligerent" countries. Thus the trade of Holland and Denmark suffered through events in Germany; the Scandinavian and Baltic countries were disadvantageously affected by the absence of trade between Western Europe and Russia, while Norway in particular was hit by the slump in shipping freights after 1920.

The case of the pound sterling, which has remained the leading European currency, and of the other currencies mentioned, will be dealt with in detail in the next chapter. The case of the French franc is as instructive in its way as that of the German paper mark.

From 1919 to early 1923 the French franc depreciated steadily but relatively slowly. At the time of the French invasion of the Ruhr it stood at between 80 and 90 to the pound. Shortly after that disastrous adventure began it broke away to 120, but was saved by the help of American financiers, by virtue of loans from whom M. Poincaré brought it back to 60. From that point it depreciated steadily and slowly again. At the beginning of 1925 it stood at 88; in the early summer it was at round about 94. Then a more rapid depreciation set in. From June to July, 1925, it fell to 108. By the end of the autumn of 1925 it fell further to 130. Just prior to the close of the year it stood at 135.

The root cause of the depreciation throughout was simply inflation, for which there was less justification than probably anywhere else in Europe, and which was persisted in simply and solely by reason of the refusal of the French people to allow themselves to be taxed to anything like the extent that obtained in this country, and their inability therefore to balance their Budget, the recurring deficits in which were made good by loans.

The expenditure financed by the inflation was to a large extent reckless and unnecessary. The reconstruction of the devastated areas is responsible for only the earlier portion of the inflation, and even here money was recklessly poured out to contractors in the belief that, as the French themselves put it, "*l'Allemagne payera tout*" ("Germany will pay it all"). Meantime, German offers of labour and material as part payment of Reparations were refused. Later, a great deal of expenditure was incurred in connexion with the invasion of the Ruhr, a war undertaken against a disarmed enemy for political reasons. But, apart from extraordinary expenditure of this character, even the ordinary expenditure provided for in the French Budget was not covered by taxation and accordingly had to be met by loans. Throughout there was a huge expenditure on armaments, in spite of the thoroughgoing disarmament of Germany as certified by Allied Control Commissions. Policies were followed which led to costly wars in Morocco and Syria. Although France professed herself unable to pay interest on her debts to the United States and Britain, she lent large sums to her various Allies in Eastern Europe for expenditure on armaments.

Through all this welter of unnecessary expenditure taxation in France remained ridiculously low as compared with Britain. Expenditure was accordingly financed by inflation, which took the form of loans. Following the refusal of New York and London to lend owing to the chaotic state of French national finance, loans were raised internally, with a consequent expansion of the note-issue of the central issuing bank, the Banque de France.

Inflation brought about, of course, the same general results as in Germany—a decline in the external value of the currency and a decline of a substantially lesser extent in its internal value. The exchange rate of the franc rose; prices rose, but by a less percentage, at any given time, than that by which the exchange rate had risen. The same difference between the external purchasing power of the franc obtained as had previously existed in the case of the mark and given rise in minds, prejudiced to the point of imbecility, to the legend that Germany was deliberately depreciating the mark. The people who had made this accusation against Germany in 1922 maintained an embarrassed silence when exactly the same thing happened to the franc.

The French public for a long time, on every occasion when a fresh fall occurred, blamed wicked foreign speculators in London, Berlin, Amsterdam, New York—anywhere, in fact, except in Paris. Following the general election of May, 1924, suspicion of the real state into which the public finances had been brought by the Bloc National under the leadership of M. Poincaré began to filter slowly into the mind of French public opinion—everywhere else this knowledge had long been common property. In 1925 M. Caillaux told his countrymen the truth about the financial position of the French State. That position, as later summed up by him at the end of 1925,[1] was that as regards internal debt France had 150 milliards of paper francs of consolidated debt, 50 milliards paper francs of other debts not immediately repayable, 100 milliards paper francs of debts due for repayment at more or less short notice ; as regards external debt, France owed approximately 200 milliards paper francs (30 to 40 milliards gold francs). Further, there existed the obligation to spend about another 20 milliards paper francs in respect of claims from the devastated areas. The French investing public thereafter steadily lost confidence in the franc, and its fall during the second half of 1925 was definitely caused by selling from Paris—by, in fact, a flight from the franc motived by the desire of the French investor to transfer his capital into foreign-currency-securities. The French Government accordingly found it increasingly difficult to borrow at home ; and neither London nor New York would lend until France showed some sign of recognizing and paying interest on the money she had already borrowed. Then, for the first time, when she required to borrow again, France showed signs of trying to come to some arrangement to pay interest on her existing external

[1] See "The Banker" of January, 1926.

debt. The subject of international indebtedness in detail is left until the last chapter; here we may anticipate by saying that in spite of an extraordinarily generous offer by Britain no definitive arrangement has yet [1] been come to by France with either Britain or the U.S.

Inability to borrow either at home or abroad need not, however, have been a final obstacle to the stabilization of the franc, for the Banque de France held a gold reserve ample to stabilize it in March, 1926, at about 130, if not at a better rate. But even instructed French public opinion looks on banking from the point of view of the peasant, and shudders at the thought of using a gold reserve for the purpose for which it was accumulated. Were the franc once stabilized, either by the use of a portion of the gold reserve or by the help of a foreign loan, it would be a simple matter to balance the Budget —simple, that is, from the financial point of view—for the rise in home prices would itself automatically diminish the burden of the internal debt. If existing taxes were properly collected, instead of being evaded alike by peasants and wealthy people, their yield would probably suffice to balance the Budget—certainly such additional taxes as were required would not be very large. The country is prosperous, there are no unemployed—foreign labour to the extent of something like three million men has immigrated into France—and French agriculture limits the quantity of imports that are required. Many of the financial problems that beset Britain and Germany in connexion with their currencies are absent. But the franc cannot be kept stable if there is inflation, and inflation there must be if Budgetary expenditure is not met out of taxation. But here we come to the crux of the whole matter. The real problem is not financial at all, but political.

To understand why the problem of the franc exists it is

[1] June, 1926.

necessary to realize that French public opinion looks on State finance from an altogether different standpoint from that generally taken in England. The Peel-Gladstone-Harcourt tradition of meeting expenditure out of revenue and regarding as impious a proposal to conceal expenditure by "wangling" the public accounts—this tradition is not merely not honoured in France, it is not understood by any politician except M. Caillaux.

Huge and unnecessary expenditure is being indulged in (Syria, Morocco, submarines, air fleet), taxation as a whole is relatively light, and above all the taxes are not being properly collected. Salaried officials and wage-earners are paying because they cannot escape, and paying heavily, when regard is had to the smallness of their incomes; but neither peasants nor wealthy financiers and industrialists are paying anything like the amounts for which they are liable under existing rates. The machinery for compelling them to make accurate returns of income is inadequate and such means as exist are not used—the peasants and the wealthy classes are strong enough to prevent it. The *petite bourgeoisie*, which is paying more than its share, is strong enough to overthrow each successive minister who proposes, by raising rates of tax, to increase their burden—thus have fallen, in the space of less than two years, Messrs. Poincaré, Clementel, Caillaux, Painlevé, Loucheur, Doumer. The various tax proposals form an excellent subject for the intrigue between political groups in which the French excel. High finance enjoys an intimate relationship with group politics, which appears scandalous to the Puritan tradition of British finance, if not to its modern practice. A Budget based on the franc at 100 is not passed until many months late, by which time the franc has fallen to 130, which upsets the calculations on which it is based—an advantage, perhaps, from the political point of view, since it was only on paper that revenue and expenditure had balanced. The deficit due to inadequate taxation and increased by the higher prices which depreciation has brought is met by inflation. As batches of short-time loans fall due and may perhaps not be renewed, a fresh crisis arises. Next taxation is proposed and—if likely to be effective—is defeated; the crisis is tided over by a fresh dose of inflation—each dose is the last—in the ultimate form of an increase in the note issue of the Banque de France. Whereupon, in due course the franc falls again.

Financial opinion in New York, London, Amsterdam, learning by experience what to expect from debates on taxation in the French Chamber, advances to the point of discounting inflation in advance. By early in 1926, when a batch of short-term loans was about to become due, New York dropped the exchange value of the franc before the dose of inflation was formally announced. Such a fall in the franc rate will of course make necessary ultimately a dose of inflation additional to that already decided on. The parallel with the mark is complete.[1]

The French Revolution of 1789 was occasioned by the refusal of the privileged classes of the time—the nobles and the clergy—to allow themselves to be taxed when the peasants and the bourgeoisie insisted that they would no longer bear the whole burden. To-day it is the peasants and the wealthy who are the privileged classes. It is not for a foreigner to predict how the French people will deal with the situation; but it is well for an Englishman to remember, when he is perplexed that so much trouble is caused by so simple a financial problem as the stabilization of the franc when an adequate gold reserve exists and a prosperous and sound national economy stands behind it, that the French banker is at heart a peasant to whom the gold reserve is an inviolable "stocking"; and stabilization means telling the *rentier*, who still dreams of the franc back near par and lower prices, that four-fifths of his

[1] See Chapter XIV, p. 161.

capital has been lost, that the capital levy which he dreads has already been made by inflation. Only a Frenchman can say when it will be safe to publish this truth. Meantime, to the Finance Minister of the day finance is primarily an aspect of group-politics : balancing the national Budget out of Revenue is not as in England an immediate and self-evident necessity assumed by all parties but one of the issues which give piquancy to political life. Public finance in France is based not on bookkeeping, but on group-politics. French history affords better precedents for a revolution than for an effective income tax.

M. Painlevé once used the phrase "the daily plebiscite of the holders of Bonds." He was referring to the fact that holders of these Bonds frequently refuse to renew when they are politically hostile to the Government, thereby causing the latter to resort to inflation in order to provide the funds with which to redeem the Bonds. The situation so created was foreseen by one of the leaders of the Cartel, which came to power in 1924, when he said, in an epigram as French in meaning as it is in style : "We have a majority of the Chamber of Deputies, but I fear, I greatly fear, that we have not got a majority of the holders of the Floating Debt."

CHAPTER XVI

THE RETURN TO GOLD

THERE is no greater contrast in financial policy than that which has obtained between France and Britain since the Armistice. France has subordinated finance to politics; and she dominates European politics while the franc falls away and shakes the foundations of parliamentary government. Britain has since 1920 pursued the path of strict financial rectitude at the cost of both her trade and her political interests; and to-day the pound stands at par with the dollar, while Britain's trade has remained for years in a slough of depression and the country slithers from one industrial crisis to another.

The achievement of parity between the pound and the dollar in 1925 and the stabilization of the German mark in 1924 were the chief events constituting the new financial equilibrium established in Europe during the years 1924–1925. With the return of sterling to gold value is bound up a similar return on the part of a number of currencies, and the stabilization of others.

The course of sterling since the war, which we are about to trace in some detail, shows in outline a decline in 1919–1920 followed by a rise in 1921–1922, at the close of which stability is attained at a purchasing power parity about 10 per cent. below Mint Par and maintained, subject to a temporary and factitious decline at the end of 1923, until early in 1925, when sterling was pushed up to Mint Par by Government action. The course followed by sterling, which was determined by the policy of the financial authorities of this country—the Treasury and the Bank of England, influenced to some extent by the opinions of the Big Five joint-stock banks and of the Money Market —has had certain important reactions on the national finances, on prices, and on trade which will then have to be considered.

Having outlined the course of sterling during the post-war period, it is best, before tracing that course in detail, to deal with the post-war Money Market, for one of the most important elements in that market, the Treasury Bill position, has exercised an important influence on the policy followed in regulating the exchange value of sterling.

On the working of the London Money Market, the effect of the process of inflation described in Chapter XII was to cause the market to be dominated by the requirements of Government finance. The most important factor in it became the Floating Debt.

The Floating Debt is that portion of the Government debt which is held by the money market, and it consisted in the main of two items: (1) Ways and Means Advances, i.e. the Government's overdraft at the Bank of England, and advances by Public Departments, and (2) Treasury Bills. Treasury bills are in effect promises by the Government to pay, of £5,000 each,[1] which mature in 3, 6, 9, or 12 months from the date of issue. They are quoted like Bank bills or Trade bills, at so much per cent. discount. Thus if the Money Market column of the newspaper quotes opposite Three Months' Treasury Bills the figures 4¾ per cent., this means that a Treasury bill for which the Government will pay the holder £5,000 in three months from now can to-day be bought for £4,040 12s. 6d. (i.e. its face value of £5,000 less interest thereon for three months at the rate of 4¾ per cent. per annum). The holder's money will for the next three months earn him the interest reckoned on whether interest rates go up or down. It will earn him interest not at 4¾ but at a higher rate, for it is 4¾ per cent. per annum on £4,040 12s. 6d., not on £5,000, a rate which works out at 5·88 per cent. Treasury bills are the favourite short-term investments of banks and discount

[1] Formerly £1,000.

houses, and any bank will always discount a British Government Treasury bill of any maturity at the rate of the day for that maturity. An important source of banking profit is accepting money from depositors at—assuming bank rate is 5 per cent.—3 per cent. on current account or 3 to 3½ per cent. on deposit account and investing it in Treasury bills at 5·88 per cent.

Before the war Treasuries were offered by tender, the highest tenders, i.e. the highest rates of discount offered, being accepted. During the latter part of the war, and up to 1921, they were "on tap" at fixed rates. In 1921 the old system of tender was reverted to and has since been maintained.

The effect of war finance was to increase the volume of Treasury bills out of all proportion to other factors in the money market. In the middle of July, 1913, the total of the Floating Debt stood at 15 million pounds. At the end of 1921 the total was 1,300 million pounds. At the end of 1922 it had been brought down to 950 millions, and later to about 750 millions, where it still stood at the end of 1925. On March 31, 1926, the Floating Debt totalled £704,296,000, of which figure Treasury bills amounted to £564,855,000, the remainder consisting of Ways and Means Advances.

The effect of so enormous an increase on the money market was that the market became dominated by the Treasury bill position. The discount rates given just above are in each case the actual rates which obtained in the middle of January, 1926. They illustrate the importance from the point of view of Government finance of the bank rate: a rise in bank rate necessitates a rise in the Treasury bill rate—otherwise the Government would not be able to sell its bills, since the banks and discount houses would be able to get relatively better rates elsewhere—and means therefore an increase in the interest which the Government has to pay out. Similarly a fall in bank rate means a fall in the cost of the day-to-day financing of the Treasury's requirements. But the process works the other way also : it is not only bank rate which affects the Treasury bill rate, but the Treasury bill rate which affects bank rate. Assume a 4 per cent. bank rate and a Treasury bill rate at $3\frac{3}{4}$ per cent. for three-months' maturities. In the event of stringency in the money market, the Treasury might find that it could not dispose of the bills it was offering. It can only dispose of them by increasing its rate. Suppose it has to increase its rate to $4\frac{3}{4}$ per cent. All other rates in the money market at once increase correspondingly, for Treasury bills form a substantial part of the supply of the investments in which the money market employs its balances. Assuming overdrafts come 1 per cent. above bank rate, the rate would be 5 per cent., but no banker is going to allow overdrafts at 5 per cent. when he can get 5·88 per cent. on a Government security. The other market rates follow the Treasury bill rate, therefore ; and bank rate is necessarily forced up too—otherwise the bank would be in the ridiculous position of discounting bills at below market rates. And since everybody in the money market knows this would happen, and the Treasury and the Bank of England work hand in hand, what would happen in practice in such a case is that as a matter of form bank rate would be moved up first and the Treasury bill rate and other rates would follow. This, in point of fact, is what did happen in December, 1925, when a rise in bank rate occurred, not because the exchange rate needed it, but because the Treasury could not sell sufficient Treasury bills on the basis of a 4 per cent. bank rate.

These were the conditions under which sterling ran its course from 1919 onwards. After the unpegging of the dollar exchange in March, 1919, sterling declined rapidly in value, despite the postponement for three years of all interest payments on Britain's debts to the U.S. Sterling in New York at one time went as low as 3·12, and after remaining between 3·50 and 3·90 during 1920, rose somewhat in 1921 and considerably in early 1922. That sterling should be higher in 1921 and 1922, years of trade depression, than during the boom of 1920 is explicable by three considerations: (*a*) Although it is correct in terms of post-war conditions to call 1920 a "boom" year, the trade figures for 1920, when recalculated in terms of 1913 prices, were far below 1913 figures. The volume of exports in 1920, compared with 1913 figures, so far from justifying the term "boom," were far below the pre-war average. The 1919–1920 "boom" was solely a price boom, in which the U.S. and other countries participated, which could not therefore turn the balance of trade sufficiently in our favour to raise the value of sterling in terms of the dollar. (*b*) While the "boom" continued, imports of raw material were made on a large scale on the assumption that it would continue for an indefinite period; these imports were mainly paid for in cash. A good deal of our exports during this period, on the other hand, were made on a credit basis. The raw material came to a large extent from the Western Hemisphere, and dollars had to be bought to pay for it; whereas to the extent to which British merchants extended credit abroad a corresponding demand for sterling did not of course come into existence. (*c*) The decline in prices during 1921–1922 was greater in Britain than in the U.S. During the latter portion of the period, in fact, prices in the U.S. were again rising, i.e. the dollar was losing in value. The continued drop in prices in Britain was simultaneously increasing the value of the pound sterling. Sterling during this period therefore gained more in value than did the dollar—we are speaking of rates of improvement, of course, not of absolute values—and accordingly its value in terms of the dollar went up.

The same causes which raised the value of the pound sterling in terms of dollars concurrently increased its gold value, since the American dollar was throughout convertible into gold. Prices in the U.S., indeed, advanced, but they remained all the time gold prices. The dollar and gold, that is to say, lost and later regained value in terms of goods at the same rate. Hence it became customary in post-war Europe to measure currency depreciation in terms of the American dollar.

The matter of the bank rate during the "boom" period, when sterling reached the low levels mentioned, deserves attention. The rate was raised in November, 1919, and again in April, 1920. How far these rises directly affected, or were intended to affect directly, the exchange value of sterling is uncertain. Certainly the bank was fully aware that a rise in bank rate then could not produce the effect on the exchanges that it would have done under pre-war conditions, for (1) the holders of foreign balances had no security as to what sterling would be worth when they wanted them back—the old equation between the pound and gold no longer obtained; (2) the Treasury bill position prevented there being assurance that there would not be further inflation. The market knew that if the holders of Treasury bills did not renew them when they became due, the Government, in order to repay them, would be forced to increase its overdraft at the Bank of England, i.e. to borrow on Ways and Means advances. Such borrowing would inflate credit, and hence currency, in the manner already described, so that although money might be tight at the minute, it was bound to become easier. Tightness of money in the money market meant that people would insist on having their Treasury bills repaid when they became due: that implied that the Government would have to borrow on ways and means advances, and that in turn meant further inflation and the consequent relative easiness of money. In other words, tightness of money would automatically bring easiness of money. The whole position revolved around the quantity of Treasury bills in existence. The demand on the part of trade for accommodation from the market did not weigh on the position so heavily as did the requirements of the Government.

Here was the vital difference between the pre-war and the 1920 position. Formerly, people who operated in the money market looked to the Bank of England's weekly return to inform them of the position. The item of private deposits in that return showed how much money there was in the market, and the ratio of the reserve to liabilities, frequently referred to in the financial columns of the Press as "the ratio," showed how far it was safe to go in the creation of credit, and therefore how far the banks were likely to go in creating it. In 1920 the money market knew that if Treasury bills were not renewed, credit would be automatically created. The whole money market position was thus dominated by the Treasury bill issue. That in turn was the ultimate reason why the raising of the bank rate could not produce the effect on the exchanges which it used to do before the war. It will be remembered that its effect was produced by the restriction of the volume of credit in existence, and thereby the making of what remained more valuable. In 1920, the raising of bank rate could not restrict the volume of credit in existence to the necessary extent or permanently, because making money tight would be automatically followed by Government borrowing on ways and means, which would make it easier again. So long as these conditions existed the raising of bank rate was inoperative to limit the creation of credit, and therefore inoperative to turn the exchanges in Britain's favour.

What the increases in the bank rate in 1919 and 1920, or at any rate the second of them, did was to diminish the volume of forward buying on borrowed money and selling on long credit terms which was a feature of that period and which was both an effect and a cause of the high rise of prices. The Bank of England has been attacked on account of these rises, but quite unjustifiably. Whatever may be said against the later deflationist policy of the Bank during the years of depression that followed 1920, there can be no question in the minds of those who were actually in business during the boom period, as distinct from those who merely wrote articles about it years afterward, that what the Bank did by raising its rate was to slacken down dangerous speculation which was sending prices to heights which the conditions of effective demand and supply did not warrant. The absurdity of the idea that the depression of 1921 was simply the result of these rises in bank rate is shown by the fact that the depression came in countries which were not affected by the British bank rate. The collapse of the boom was due to exhaustion of the world's purchasing power at the prices then obtaining; and if bank rate had not been raised when it was, the collapse would have had far more disastrous effects than it did have in liquidations and bankruptcies. The real criticism is that the second rise ought to have come months before it did; such a warning signal would have put an end earlier to the speculations of foolish business men whose lack of foresight led them to imagine that boom conditions could last indefinitely in a war-impoverished world.

The rises in bank rate in 1919 and 1920 only influenced the exchanges indirectly by producing higher interest rates all round, and to that extent checking speculation and limiting the creation of commercial credit. The point, however, is that the requirements of the Government were so large compared to the requirements of the ordinary commercial trader, that the amount of limitation which the raising of the bank rate could enforce was nothing like sufficient to produce any appreciable effect on the total volume of credit, and therefore on the volume of our currency. The raising of the bank rate in 1920 was justified in that it tended to eliminate the speculative element which was forcing prices up to dangerous heights. But it did not, could not, and was not expected to produce the effect on the foreign exchanges which before the war it would have produced.

Early in 1922 sterling was standing at round about 4·40, and a comparison of price levels showed that that figure represented approximately its purchasing power parity. The rise in value had been accomplished as a result of the fall in sterling prices from the middle of 1920 onwards, which had been greater than the corresponding fall in dollar prices. This price deflation would not, however, have been possible without the reduction in the Floating Debt, which took place during this period—from 1,300 to 950 millions—which in turn rendered possible a lesser volume of circulating currency. That volume was in fact reduced as shown in the following Table: [1]

Date	Amount of Currency Note Issue (in million pounds)	Gold (Coin and Bullion) held against Currency (in Notes million pounds
Dec. 30th, 1914	38	18½
,, ,, 1915	103	28½
,, ,, 1916	150	28½
,, ,, 1917	212	28½
,, ,, 1918	323	28½
June 25th, 1919	342	28½
Dec. 31st, 1919	356	28½
,, 29th, 1920	364	28½
,, 28th, 1921	323	28½
Mar. 29th, 1922	298	28½
June 28th, 1922	294	28½
Dec. 27th, 1922	300	27

[1] This process of price inflation threw into the background the question of direct monetary deflation dealt with by the Cunliffe Committee in 1918–1919. That Committee recommended the gradual calling in and cancelling of currency notes until the pound sterling had been

From early 1922 onwards sterling remained round about 4·40, apart from a small and unjustified fall in the winter of 1923, which arose out of political causes and which was soon recovered, down to the early part of 1925. Then came the return to gold; sterling was brought up to parity with the dollar.

Since July, 1923, bank rate had stood at 4 per cent. During the first months of 1925 sterling, in anticipation of the return to gold, mounted steadily towards parity with the dollar. Early in March the Federal Reserve rate having been raised from 3 per cent. to 3½ per cent., bank rate was raised from 4 per cent. to 5 per cent., the object being to retain American floating balances in London in preparation for the return to gold. The Chancellor of the Exchequer in his Budget speech next month announced the Government's intention to return immediately to the gold standard. The law prohibiting the export of gold, which expired that year, would not be renewed. A loan had been arranged in New York specifically for the purpose of supporting the exchange rate; it was hoped and believed its use would not be necessary, but it would be available if required. The free gold market had been restored, but for the time being the existing embargo on the raising of foreign loans in London was maintained, in order that fresh claims on sterling should not be created.[1] There was a tacit understanding among London bullion dealers that gold should not be sent abroad in connexion with exchange transactions. The results of these measures was

brought to its par value as measured by the dollar exchange: in other words, a policy of gradual monetary deflation. That policy was not carried out to the extent to which its more convinced advocates thought desirable. The cancelling of currency notes could only have been accomplished if there had been a sufficient surplus of income over expenditure. Without this monetary deflation was impossible. The main lines of the Committee's policy were, however, adopted, in particular the limitation of the fiduciary circulation of currency notes (i.e. that portion not backed by gold or by Bank of England notes). But the main element in deflation was the price deflation referred to above, accompanied by the reduction in the volume of the Floating Debt.

[1] See Chapter IX.

that the efflux of gold threatened by the lapse of the prohibition on export was turned into an influx, and sterling mounted steadily up from 4·80, passed the lower gold point, and reached over 4·85. Early in August, 1925, bank rate was reduced to 4½ per cent. Thereafter an efflux of gold set in to Batavia, occasioned by the need to finance the Dutch colony's rubber exports. In spite of this efflux, bank rate was further reduced to 4 per cent. in October. The motive of these reductions is obscure: perhaps it was economic rather than financial, a concession to those who maintained that the high bank rate was retarding trade. In November the embargo was lifted. The lifting of the embargo signifies the real restoration of the gold standard. In December, 1925, the bank rate was raised once more to 5 per cent., owing to the exigencies of the national finances, the Government finding an increasing difficulty in selling the Treasury bills necessary to provide the money for its day-to-day requirements at rates corresponding to a 4 per cent. bank rate.

The policy followed since the war had been the gradual restoration of the pound to its par value, and this policy reached its culmination in 1925. The position from the point of view of Mint regulations is that the bank must buy all gold bullion offered to it at the price of £3 17s. 9d. per standard ounce, i.e. per ounce $\frac{11}{16}$ fine; while holders of legal tender can demand gold bars—but not, as before the war, gold coin—in exchange for their legal tender at the rate of £3 17s. 10½d. per standard ounce.[1] The only check to an uncovered issue of £1 and 10/- notes consists in the Treasury Minute of December 15, 1919,[2] which limited the maximum fiduciary issue for any given year—by "fiduciary issue" is meant an issue not covered by gold—to the maximum actual fiduciary issue for the preceding year.

The policy of returning to the gold standard was that of

[1] See Gregory "The Return of Gold." [2] *Ibid.*

the Treasury and the Bank of England, and it had the general support of banking opinion, to which there were, however, important qualifications and exceptions. The last decisive step, the pushing up of the pound to Mint Par in 1925, was strongly criticized both before and after it had been taken. Mr. McKenna expressed grave doubts beforehand as to its wisdom, and the Federation of British Industries repeatedly expressed the opinion that there was a great danger in expediting the return to gold. Sir Josiah Stamp was of the same opinion, and Professor J. M. Keynes was definitely against the policy of the return to gold, his alternative being a currency "managed" by the authorities with a view to keeping prices stable—which, if it could be attained by this means, would, on the hypothesis of purchasing power parity, automatically keep exchange rates steady. In view of these expressions of opinion and of the fact that the financial and economic situation of the country at the present time is definitely affected by the return to gold it is necessary to review the various considerations affecting the policy followed.

A great deal of the controversy has been at cross-purposes by reason of the failure to distinguish between four separate issues. These may be distinguished as follows: Was it or was it not desirable—

(1) To raise bank rate in 1920?
(2) To have as an ultimate aim the return of the pound to the gold standard?
(3) To try to realize that aim by a policy of gradual deflation?
(4) To push the pound up from 4·40 to Mint Par in 1925?

Issue (1) has no real connexion with the other three. Whatever the Bank's motive may have been, the raising of the rate in April, 1920, would have been not only desirable but necessary quite apart from any question of ultimately returning to the gold standard, in order to put a check to the buying on borrowed money and selling on long credit at prices quite unjustified by the conditions of supply and effective demand which obtained during the speculative boom. If the rate had not been raised, the boom might have gone on longer and its collapse would have been so much the more disastrous. The raising of bank rate was justified quite apart from the consideration of an ultimate return to the gold standard.

(2) The desirability of the gold standard in itself was hardly questioned prior to the war, and post-war experience has confirmed that opinion. The ardent desire to return thereto on the Continent was born of experience of what happened in its absence. Its salient advantage lies in its relative stability: the amount of gold available cannot suddenly be increased, and gold prices cannot therefore change suddenly. Gold, while by no means absolutely stable in value, is stable relatively to the fluctuations in value of other commodities. The supply cannot be suddenly increased or diminished. In this respect it stands in the greatest contrast to paper money, which can be printed *ad infinitum* by any government. A gold basis to a currency, again, is a far simpler arrangement than would be the basing of currency on the exchange value of wheat or other commodities. In any case, on whichever side the balance of theoretical advantage may be, the fact remains that before the war the gold basis worked very well by reason of the fact that everywhere in the world people do, as a matter of fact, want gold. Everywhere in the civilized world people will, as a matter of fact, take gold under any circumstances. A man in New York with a bag of sovereigns could always go to the U.S. Treasury and get them changed for dollars at the par rate. When sterling drafts were being sold for $3·90 a man with sovereigns in New York could always get $4.8665 for each sovereign. Some people have made it their business to

attack this preference for gold as unreasonable. It may be. It may be a fact, as Mr. Hartley Withers once suggested, that people only want gold because every one else wants it. However that may be, the preference itself, and with it the fact that the volume of gold in existence cannot be suddenly increased, were facts sufficiently strong to have induced all the principal commercial countries of Europe and America before the war to adopt the gold basis. The " managed " currency advocated by Mr. J. M. Keynes and by certain groups on the political left may not be impracticable. The objection to it is that it would offer an inducement, where the gold standard raises a barrier, to exploitation for political ends. If it were " managed " by devotees of pure finance, such as Mr. Keynes, it would undoubtedly be ideal. The present writer, certainly, would willingly live under so enlightened and benevolent a despotism. But we know that, under modern political conditions, it would not in fact be so managed, but would be operated in the interest of whatever groups could obtain control of the machinery of the State. Post-war experience most indubitably confirms the desirability of removing the temptation to juggle with currency from governments, and the gold standard makes such juggling more difficult than it would otherwise be. Political ends, however desirable they may be, are best pursued by political methods, not by currency manipulation. Britain, which can feed herself only for a few weeks in the year, is the last country in the world to take risks with the currency that purchases her wheat and meat. A country such as France, with a peasant population and a home food supply, can afford to take risks which our wholly industrialized country dare not incur.

The further objection to the gold standard—that it necessitates a higher bank rate than would otherwise be necessary—is probably true under present-day conditions. To this extent it constitutes an objection to making the return at the time when it was made, but it is not an objection to the gold standard under all conditions. The hardship inflicted on traders by a ½ per cent. or 1 per cent. rise in bank rate affects only those who finance their business on short-term borrowed money in the form of bills of exchange, overdrafts, and acceptances; and even so the amount of hardship inflicted on traders is very small. The real sufferers by a rise in bank rate are the bill-brokers, not the traders in commodities. It cannot be contended that under pre-war conditions such rises in bank rates as occurred inflicted any very appreciable hardship; certainly in those times it was not seriously suggested that the gold standard should be given up on that account. The real force of the argument against the gold standard from the rises in bank rate which it from time to time necessitates applies only to the return to gold under the conditions of 1925, not to the general aim of ultimately returning to gold.

(3) The desirability of the gold standard may thus fairly be held to justify the authorities in following the policy of re-establishing it, but it does not absolve them from having seriously erred in the measures actually taken to carry out the policy—quite apart from the issue whether the final step taken in 1925 ought or ought not to have been postponed, to which we shall come in a moment. In saying this we are not associating ourselves with the argument that deflation is responsible for the high degree of unemployment which has been continuous in Britain since the collapse of the boom. If the deflation that took place before 1925 rendered it more difficult for countries with depreciated currencies to buy our goods, the fall in prices made possible by decreased costs of labour and raw material rendered it easier. Deflation implied cheaper food, cheaper manufacturing costs, and—above all—an increased credit power to finance foreign trade. The importance of the last consideration cannot be exaggerated

from the point of view of taking the lead in the reconstruction of Europe, with the benefits to this country which that leadership implies. The reason for the unemployment of the years following 1920 is the general exhaustion of the world's purchasing power, owing to the destruction of wealth during the war. The "boom" of 1919–1920 was only an interlude, due in the first instance to the necessity for replacing stocks and the desire to spend profits made during the war; then the rise in prices led to speculative activity. If this activity had not been checked by rises in the bank rate there would have been many more failures in the liquidation of the following years; for when the war-profits were spent and the stocks replaced the "boom" had to come to an end. The purchasing power necessary to sustain a flourishing export trade did not, and does not, exist; it was destroyed between 1914 and 1918. The number of our unemployed corresponds roughly to the increase in population since 1913, and this "high" figure of unemployment—"high" compared with pre-war times—is probably one of the "normal" features of the post-war era. It is true that in Germany a depreciating currency temporarily stimulated exports and resulted in a very small degree of unemployment, and similarly in France and Belgium. But—apart from the instability of the situation there—the small degree of unemployment is only possible by reason of the fact that the great mass of the workers of those nations have, unwillingly or willingly, accepted a very much lower standard of life than before the war. In England, on the contrary, many classes of the population are enjoying about the same standard as in 1914. That large numbers of others are unemployed is the corollary of this. Even the lower standard of life in Germany did not prevent unemployment figures there far exceeding the British, when stabilization came. The pound, the mark and the franc illustrate the error of supposing that a long war need not be paid for by the mass of the population, if only you know how to juggle with currencies and prices. Industrial nations, depending on exports for their livelihood, are left to choose between the total impoverishment of some and the partial impoverishment of all.

The only means whereby this state of affairs can be ameliorated is the establishment abroad of conditions under which the European countries and their overseas customers can gradually recover their purchasing power.

A further consideration in favour of the policy of deflation until the gold standard was restored is the fact that the interest on our debt to the U.S. and repayments of the principal thereof have to be paid in dollars.[1] The more dollars sterling will purchase the less the burden of the debt becomes. It is of course true that ultimately this debt, like Reparations, can only be paid in goods. But depreciation tends, as we have seen,[2] to bring about a gap between purchasing power parity and exchange rates, and the burden of the debt would be heavier by the extent of this gap.

The real criticism against the authorities on their policy of deflation is that they seem never to have really faced the fact that a policy of deflation would make the burden of the enormous war debt heavier. Nearly half the national expenditure goes in interest on the war debt; and every step taken on the road to deflation made the pound more valuable and therefore increased the burden of the war-loan, interest and, indeed, the burden of debts of every kind. It was utterly against the interests of the Exchequer that it should have made this present to the *rentier* class. Deflation implied a levy to reduce or extinguish the war-debt—either a levy on war wealth or a general capital levy, or both. In the absence of such a levy the burden of the interest on the war-debt, increased by deflation, falls on the taxpayer and through him on industry and the manual working and salaried classes—on the younger generation

[1] See Chapter XVIII. [2] See Chapter XIII.

generally. If, for political reasons a levy were decided to be undesirable then the policy of deflation ought never to have been followed and the pound ought on the collapse of the post-war boom to have been left to find its own level.

(4) The gold standard was on this view desirable in itself: the policy of deflation would have been sound had it been accompanied by a levy on capital. Was the return to the gold standard in 1925, given the actual conditions then obtaining, a wise step? It can hardly be doubted in the light of experience that it was not, and that it gratuitously added to Britain's difficulties.

At the end of 1924 the pound stood round about 4·40, at which figure, apart from a slight and quite temporary relapse at the end of 1923, it had stood since 1922. Price deflation had brought the pound from below 4 dollars to within 10 per cent. of Mint Par. Practical stability had been attained, without Government support, on the basis of purchasing power parity. A fall in American prices, or a rise in English prices, would indeed have caused the pound to decline again; but there was no reason to anticipate either. A rise in American prices, or a further fall in English prices, on the other hand, would have taken the pound higher still; a fall of 10 per cent. in English prices would have brought it to Mint Par. Such a fall might have come about over the next few years by natural means had intensive Government and municipal economy reduced taxes and rates and had employers and employed co-operated to increase efficiency, i.e. had costs of production declined. The Treasury's object of a return to Mint Par would have come about as the natural result of Government economy and national efficiency. The Floating Debt would have been enabled to be consolidated in great part by a long-term loan.

Such was the attitude of those who, outside the circles of the Treasury and the Bank, confessed to a desire to see the return to the gold standard. Deflation, which was to be accompanied by a levy on capital for the wiping out of the war-debt, was to be effected by governmental economy and increased production.

Such a natural but slow process was not to the liking of the Treasury. Instead of allowing the pound to rise gradually and naturally, and confining themselves to creating the conditions favourable to such a rise, it pushed the pound up suddenly from 4·40 to par in the manner described above. Exchange rate and purchasing power parity no longer coincided. The exchange rate of the pound was 10 per cent. higher than its purchasing value. The immediate result was a worsening of the export trades. Goods which could have been sold in Belgium with the pound worth 94 francs were unsaleable when it was worth 104. Imported raw materials, indeed, became correspondingly cheaper, but they represent only part of the manufacturers' costs; labour costs and overhead charges remained the same.

The Treasury seem to have acted in the belief that prices would automatically fall as the exchange value of the pound rose. The restriction of credit which follows the raising of bank rate would, in theory, mean the liquefying of stocks by throwing them on the market; prices of manufactured goods would fall, while prices of imported food and materials would already have fallen by reason of their lower cost in pounds. Wages and the cost of living would be reduced. Ultimately, a new equilibrium would be arrived at, with prices and wages 10 per cent. lower than before. In theory this is what should have happened. Pre-war, no doubt, it would have done; in practice in 1925 it did not. The theory of the well-balanced world of 1913 frequently does not work in the dislocated world after the war. The rings and combinations both inside and outside Britain, the power of American producers and English retailers, prevented various prices from falling by 10 per cent.; the trade unions in the sheltered industries (e.g. the railways) were able to prevent wages from taking the initiative downward. The export trades, indeed, were forced by foreign competition to lower prices to the extent that the pound had risen, but the attempt of one of them to lower wage costs produced a crisis which led to the coal subsidy. The coal crisis would indeed probably have come anyhow, for coal was in a bad position before the return to the gold standard, but the crisis was undoubtedly made more acute thereby. The situation of the export trades would have been hopeless were it not that the effect of the return to the gold standard in increasing their sterling prices to foreign buyers was to some extent offset by cheap subsidized coal. The year closed with an enormous adverse visible balance of trade never previously equalled and with the export trades, despite the coal subsidy, in a worse position than ever, in many cases, compared with those of other countries.

The adverse balance of trade should, in theory, have led by way of restricted credit and an outflow of gold, to lower prices and wages at home, and thus ultimately have remedied the situation. But the outflow of gold and the restriction of credit were prevented until November, 1925, by the embargo on foreign loans, which obviated the necessity of making a number of payments abroad. With the removal of the embargo and the absence of a sufficient supply of gold to make possible substantial gold exports one must expect a restriction of credit and a decline in prices. The general level of wholesale prices had indeed fallen by the end of 1925 to a level corresponding approximately to the existing exchange rate, but some share in this fall is to be ascribed to the coal subsidy. Retail prices had not fallen to anything like 10 per cent., nor had wages. Manufacturers' costs, both labour costs and overhead charges, had not fallen to any appreciable extent; in fact, the process of adjusting manufacturing costs to a par exchange had by the end of 1925 scarcely begun. And even if retail prices were ultimately to follow wholesale prices in a 10 per cent. decline, it is not at all certain that wages in the sheltered trades would follow them. If in the end they do not, then real wages, i.e. real manufacturing costs, will have been increased.

The general level of prices and wages must indeed ultimately come down to a par exchange, but it may well be that this will be accomplished, not by a 10 per cent. fall all round, but by a bigger fall in the case of trades exposed to foreign competition and a very slight fall only in other trades.

The results of the return to gold have thus been :

(1) A worsening in the position of the export trades, including coal.

(2) The making of a present of the fall in prices to the *rentier* class at the expense of industry—at the expense, that is, of employers and employed alike.

(3) A widening of the gap between sheltered and unsheltered industries.

The effects have thus been exactly opposite to those which statemanship would have desired to produce in Britain in 1925.

It is true that, as against these disadvantages, stability of the value of the pound in terms of gold has been achieved, and dependence on a shifting purchasing power parity eliminated. This is to the good as far as it goes, but the force of this consideration is substantially weakened by the fact that dependence on the dollar has not been eliminated. The Federal Reserve loan has not indeed been used ; but the fact remains that it was thought desirable to have such a loan. Bank rate itself is as dependent on the Federal Reserve rate as it was before the return ; the discount houses still habitually "watch New York." A sharp drop in American prices, i.e. a sharp rise in the value of the dollar ; or a sharp rise in the Federal Reserve

Bank's interest rate, which would cause a transfer of floating balances to New York (see Chapter X); either might conceivably bring the pound so considerably below the lower gold point that the Bank's gold reserve would be threatened. In that case, it would remain to be seen whether sterling were intrinsically strong enough for a sharp rise in bank rate to lift the rate again above the lower gold points. Such a rise, with the consequent rise in interest rates all round, would increase costs once more. Sterling is still semi-dependent on the dollar.

Even so, the gold standard cannot be regarded as absolutely secure. A substantial revival in trade is indeed highly unlikely for an indefinite period, but supposing it should come, e.g. as the result of a war in which England, taught by experience, remained neutral, the building up of stocks would become necessary and prices would rise. More money would be required by trade. The rate of discount and the rate of interest for loans and overdrafts would rise, and here, it seems, would be felt the fatal weakness of the Floating Debt. Holders of Treasury bills, finding a more remunerative use for their money, would fail to renew them. The Government would be forced to increase its Treasury bill rates. It is a question whether the resources of the money market would suffice for both Government and trade requirements. If they did not, either a certain amount of trade would become impossible owing to lack of credit accommodation or the Government would have to borrow on Ways and Means Advances, or both. If the Government borrowed substantially on Ways and Means Advances the process of inflation would recommence; prices would rise faster in Britain than in the U.S. by reason of this element of inflation, the exchange might move below the lower gold point at a rate which the gold shipments which it would be within the Bank of England's power to make would be inadequate to hold in check. The gold standard would then be endangered.

The danger is not a present one, for the considerable revival of trade which it postulates is not in sight, or even likely, apart from unforeseen political circumstances. In the meantime a 5 per cent. bank rate, which the gold standard seems to be likely frequently to necessitate, although its effect in hindering trade is often exaggerated, is certainly an additional burden on industry which is felt at a time when so many businesses are being run on small margins or on no margins at all, and also increases the burden of the Floating Debt on the National Exchequer. The crux of the position is the Floating Debt. If the aim is to be the maintenance of the gold standard, it is essential that the Treasury bill position should cease to carry its present weight in the money market; in other words, that the Government's requirements should be further reduced. The difficulty of the situation is that many items of expenditure are automatically increasing.

The salient fact in connexion with the return to gold was that the processes which brought it about were entirely financial in character. It was not a case of public and private economy and efficient production having created an increasing total trade balance. It was a case first of purchasing power parity coming down to meet the sterling rate of exchange through British prices falling while those in the U.S. fell more slowly and finally rose; then, of high rates of interest in London attracting U.S. balances and retaining them. These financial operations of the British Treasury were, as financial operations, well considered and successful in result. But they were unaccompanied by any improvement in the net trade balance; on the contrary, the trade position has during the last few years become steadily worse. In 1913 there was, according to the Board of Trade calculation, a favourable net trade balance, after allowing for invisible exports, of 181 millions. In 1923 this had shrunk to 153 millions. The drop, the full importance of which is only realized when we remember how much less money was worth in 1923 than in 1913, is partly to be ascribed to the decline in the item of interest on capital invested abroad owing to the selling of so many of these securities to the U.S. to pay for munitions and food during the war. In 1924 the net trade balance had shrunk from its 1923 figure of 153 millions to 63 millions. In 1915 it was only 29 millions. It is arguable that the decline in the interest derived from overseas investments justified a permanent levelling down of the pound below par. In any case, to increase the value of a country's currency by financial operations during the period of a declining trade balance needs more justification than the vague hope of a trade revival.

The criticism of the Treasury's action may be summed up by saying that the return to the gold standard was not justified at the time when it took place. A gold standard is a luxury, justified in a certain state of prosperity and rightly postulated as an aim of national policy, but not suited to the impoverished condition of post-war Britain in 1925. Britain's financial dress should suit her reduced circumstances. The assumption of parity with the dollar is merely pretending to be better off than she is—an artificial sunburn.

CHAPTER XVII

STABILIZATION

THE return of the pound to the gold standard was only one, although one of the two most important, of the stabilizations of currencies which took place generally during the years 1924–1925, and which, taken all together, constituted in effect the creation of a new equilibrium in international finance.

These stabilizations took in general one of three forms :

(*a*) The return to a free gold market. Sweden took this step shortly before Britain, Holland and the Union of South Africa at the same time, Australia and New Zealand shortly afterwards.

(*b*) The issue of a new currency at par value with the pound or the dollar, and maintained at that value, without a free gold market, by control of exchange transactions by the authorities. This was the case of the German gold mark ; also of the Latvian gold lat, the Austrian schilling, the Hungarian krone, the Russian chervonetz.

Particulars of the new currencies and their relations to the currency which existed before the inflation destroyed its value are given in the currency tables contained in Chapter II. In the case of Poland the new currency unit, the zloty, had by the end of 1925 proved unable to maintain itself ; early in 1926 it was round about 30, and Poland was asking for assistance from abroad.

(*c*) The stabilizing of the depreciated currency at a fixed point below parity by Government control of exchange dealings, as in the case of the Belgian franc, the Italian lira, and the Esthonian paper mark. The same course had already been effectually followed in the case of the Czecho-Slovak krone and the Finnish mark. The various rates at which stabilization was effected appear in the tables above referred to.

The actual procedure of stabilizing a currency is simple, if the resources are there. A government or central banking institution possessing a reserve of gold, or of foreign stable-value currency (dollars, pounds), or disposing of foreign credits in the shape of the right to draw up to a certain figure on the Federal Reserve Bank of New York or the Bank of England—a government or central banking institution in these circumstances has only to instruct its exchange brokers to buy all drafts in its own currency which are offered for sale below a certain price, the funds to pay for such purchases being the gold, or the dollars or pounds, which it has in reserve, or the foreign bank credits on which it can and does draw. The mere fact that all of the drafts in the currency which is being stabilized which come on to the foreign exchange market find a ready sale at a certain figure keeps the currency at that figure, i.e. stabilizes the rate. Of course, the process is only effective so long as the reserve or the credits hold out and if the figure chosen as the stabilization rate is such, given actual balance of payments over a period, as the currency can reasonably be expected to maintain once a barrier has been put up against the cumulative effect of past inflation. If that condition is not justified, if, e.g., the rate chosen is more favourable than is justified by the payments which the country has to make on trade or on loan account or by the extent of past inflation, then the currency will fall away again from the rate at which it was attempted to be stabilized, as happened when M. Poincaré tried to stabilize the French franc at 60.

The way in which a government acquires the control of gold or foreign currency sufficient to enable it to stabilize an inflated currency is generally that of a foreign loan. The process outlined under (*b*) and (*c*) above were in some cases made possible by foreign loans, in others (Germany, Russia) stabilization and the issue of a new currency were carried out by the country concerned without foreign help.

In the cases of Germany and Italy, foreign loans followed the stabilization. The importance of the stabilizing influence of the loans granted by U.S. and British bankers came out strikingly in the case of the Belgian franc. In the latter part of 1925 the Belgian Government made a very advantageous debt settlement with the U.S. on a 55 per cent. basis, and the debts to Britain and France having already been settled, nothing appeared to stand in the way of a stabilizing loan from U.S. and British bankers, for which the Belgian Government proceeded to negotiate. The fact of the negotiations was known, and the Belgian Government had no difficulty in holding the franc steady at round about 107. In the middle of March the franc suddenly fell from 107 to 119 in one day. Then it came out that there was a hitch in the negotiations, the bankers having demanded, *inter alia*, that the Belgian State railways charge remunerative rates, as the German railways are forced to do under the Dawes Plan, in place of low rates, the deficiency in which is made good by a State subsidy. It was at once clear that the possibility of stabilizing the Belgian franc permanently depended on satisfying U.S. and British bankers.[1]

The details of the most important and most difficult of the stabilizations that have been carried out, that of the German mark, have already been given in Chapter XIV. If we desire, on the basis of our experience of the mark and other stabilized currencies, to generalize as to what happens when stabilization takes place, subject, of course, to the special circumstances of each case, we may sum up as follows :

One technical objection brought against stabilization, the difference between the internal and the external value of a depreciated currency, does not hold, as experience has shown that, if stabilization can once be accomplished, this

[1] The dependence of the Belgian franc on the French franc is due to the fact that Belgium, since the War, has moved politically within the French orbit.

difference is only temporary; the internal price level rises to a general equality with the fixed exchange rate. As regards the exchange value of such a currency at the time when the adverse influences cease to be operative, it is probable that where the past inflation has been considerable, the exchange value will for some time be less than purchasing power parity, by reason of the secondary effect of inflation in lowering the credit of the issuing country. In so far as the loss of exchange value is due to the discounting of a supposedly unfavourable future, it may be expected to be recovered when the adverse influences cease to be operative. As regards prices, it is likely that the effects of past inflation will require some time to work themselves out. The probability is, therefore, that even after exchange values have recovered somewhat, there will still remain a gap between them and purchasing power parity. But two forces will be at work to close it. On the one hand, prices will be moving upwards towards a new level determined by the extent of past inflation, the supply of commodities available, and the velocity of circulation of the currency. On the other hand, the fact that exchange values are lower than purchasing power parity will, as we have seen earlier, enable exporters for some time longer to undersell their rivals abroad. The resulting export boom will, other things being equal and in the absence of further inflation, create abroad a demand for the currency in question in order to pay for these goods, and this demand will send up the exchange value of the currency. These two forces will, in the absence of other disturbing factors, tend to close up the gap between the internal and the external value of the currency. As the two values approach one another, the export boom will slacken, for the rise in prices will pull wages and salaries after it, and costs of production will rise; exporters will have continually to revise their price-lists upwards. Finally, when exchange rates approximate to purchasing power parity, the two processes will stop. For, on the one hand, there will be no further inducement for the prices of the goods entering into international trade to rise since they have reached the level of world-prices; while on the other, the exchange value of the currency will no longer tend to appreciate, since export prices will no longer be artificially cheap to foreigners. What remains of the export boom will die away and be replaced by competition on a more or less equal footing. The general level of home prices may perhaps take a little longer to adjust itself to the new equilibrium; and the difficulties which usually follow a boom may be expected to make their appearance: liquidations, unemployment, and unrest. From this stage of more or less normal competition onward, exchange rates will fluctuate within relatively narrow limits round purchasing power parity. In the absence of some new disturbing factor, such as fresh inflation, large reparations or war-debts repayments, or political events, the balance of trade and interest payments will rule exchange rates, perhaps keeping rates and purchasing power parity steady, perhaps causing them to move slowly together in one direction or the other. In either case the direction would depend on such factors as the nature of the political settlement and the debt settlement, natural advantages, standards of life, real wages, and the productivity of labour; it would no longer be primarily a currency question.

It is necessary to guard against the error of supposing that the return to gold and stabilization are equivalent to a return to pre-war conditions. For one thing, the return to gold is not universal: there are still depreciated currencies which have not been stabilized at all, of which the most prominent at the moment of writing is the French franc. Again, there are other depreciated currencies which have been stabilized at far below par value, such as the Italian lira and the Czecho-Slovak krone. Further, of the new currencies which were issued at par, one, the Polish zloty, has failed to maintain that value and has depreciated substantially. Even in the case of the others—the German gold mark, the Russian chervonetz—parity is maintained only by the exercise of control on the part of the authorities. Only in London, Amsterdam, and Stockholm, of all the monetary centres of Europe, is there a free gold market in the sense in which such a market formerly existed generally in Europe. The free flow of gold between the principal monetary centres of of the world which obtained in pre-war days no longer exists. Most of these centres no longer possess sufficient gold to permit of such a flow taking place, for half the world's available supply is in New York. The return to gold is real enough, in the sense that most of the depreciated currencies have either been restored to parity with gold or anchored more or less firmly at a definite point below parity: but the gold exchange basis on which the new equilibrium rests is very different from the free gold market of pre-war days.

The full significance of the return to gold will, however, best be realized after we have dealt with the relation between existing international debts and the exchange position.

CHAPTER XVIII

INTERNATIONAL DEBTS

WE have seen, in the example of the Belgian and the French franc, that the possibility of stabilizing an inflated currency depends on satisfying U.S. and British bankers as to the state of the national finances. Hence the importance to the exchanges of the matter of international debts, for foreign loans must be preceded by settlements of existing obligations. American and British bankers will not lend to governments which, like the French, fail to settle already-existing debts. Stabilization depends on debt settlements.

The general stabilizing of the European currencies has accordingly been accompanied by settlements—temporary settlements, at all events—of the matter of international debts. The terms of these settlements require consideration. The subject is directly relevant to foreign exchange, not only for the reason just given, but also because the payment of interest and repayment of principal create a demand for the currency in which the payments have to be made; they tend, therefore, to send up the value of that currency and to send down the value of the currency of the country which is making the payment, in the manner set out in Chapter VII. The fact that such payments have to be made is known and is apt to be discounted in advance. If default is made in making payment, the currency of the defaulting country is likely to suffer by reason of the effect on its credit.

The matter at issue is best considered separately under two heads: debts incurred by borrowing between nations which were allied during the war, and Reparations. We are dealing here, it will be remembered, only with debts owed by one State to another State. Loans made by banking and accepting institutions, money subscribed by the public to share or debenture issues or to public loans in another country do not come into the question.

As regards Reparations, no figure was fixed at the Peace Conference in 1919. The ridiculous figure of 6,600 millions was fixed at the Brussels Conference in 1921, when it was also settled that payments made by Germany should be divided up in the following proportions: France 50 per cent., Britain 22 per cent., Italy 8 per cent., others 20 per cent. During 1922 Germany's payments were made on the basis settled provisionally at the Cannes Conference. This scheme had been arranged to last for a year only, and expired in January, 1923. A further "Allied" conference was held at Paris to determine payments for the following year, at which a practicable scheme was submitted by the British Treasury experts, but M. Poincaré contemptuously refused to discuss it in order to be free to carry out the already-planned invasion of the Ruhr. French hostilities against the disarmed inhabitants lasted through the great part of 1923, during which time no Reparations were paid, apart from seizures of coal, etc., by the French. During the French occupation a committee was appointed, called the Dawes Committee, to determine the utmost that Germany could pay. The Dawes Committee reported in 1924 and its report was accepted by all the powers concerned at the London Conference of 1924 and made the basis of the Reparations payments since. Briefly, the Dawes Scheme provided that Germany should make payments as follows:

	Million £
1st year - - - - -	50
2nd " - - - - -	61
3rd " - - - - -	60
4th " - - - - -	87½
5th " and subsequently -	125

The 125 millions to be paid during the "normal" year is subject to increase according to a complicated index of prosperity—i.e. if Germany's national income, calculated in a given way, rises above a certain figure, the 125 millions is to be increased by a certain percentage. If, however, the national income falls below the stated figure, the 125 millions have to be paid all the same.

For the convenience of the reader, the figures are given in terms of pounds; the official figures are in gold marks.

The sums named have to be handed over by Germany in marks to an official called the Agent-General for Reparations, upon whom, assisted by a body called the Transfer Committee, lies the responsibility of transferring them into the currencies of the recipients in such a way that the stability of the external value of the mark, i.e. its exchange rate, shall not be endangered.

Of the sums named, half are to be provided by the German Budget, half by revenue derived from the railways, from debentures on German industries, and from certain specified taxes on tobacco, alcohol, beer, sugar, and customs duties.

Up to the time of writing,[1] only the first complete year under the Dawes Scheme has elapsed. During that year Germany paid 47 millions, of which 40 millions came, as provided by the Dawes Scheme, out of a loan made to Germany specifically for that purpose and to assist her in reorganizing her finances after the disasters of the Ruhr invasion and the inflation.

By the beginning of 1926 it had become clear to all unprejudiced observers that the Dawes Commission, once more, had vastly over-estimated German capacity to pay. However the fact may be disguised, it remains true that Reparations can only be paid out of a favourable balance of trade, and such balance did not exist at the end of 1925, and although it may come into existence in due course, it is not within the bounds of economic probability that, if it does, it will amount to sufficient to enable Germany to

[1] June, 1926.

pay anything like the 125 millions per annum payable under the Dawes Scheme.

A review of the position as it existed early in 1926, based on the Agent-General's Report for the period up to the end of 1925, will make this clear, and will show how by early in 1926 the application of the Dawes Plan had already operated to prolong and intensify the stabilization crisis.

The stabilization crisis has already been described (Chapter XIV). The salient features of that crisis as it developed in the second half of 1925 were unemployment on a vast scale (1½ millions by the end of 1925 rising to over 2 millions in early 1926); shortage of liquid capital; high rates of interest; high taxation; a continuous stream of bankruptcies far above the pre-war average; widespread inability to compete in the world's markets; an adverse trade balance. To sum up, British conditions intensified and worsened, accompanied by a much lower general standard of living.

These conditions, it may be repeated, were not in the first instance created by the Dawes Scheme; they were the effects of stabilization. But they were intensified by the Dawes Scheme, which also prevented them from being alleviated. Taxation was far higher than it would otherwise have been, thus intensifying the inability to compete. Railway tariffs, which were called on to furnish part of the funds from which the Dawes payments were to be made, were kept at a level which increased costs all round. Rates of interest were maintained at a high level when a policy of alleviation would have lowered them as far as possible consistently with the avoidance of inflation; the Reichsbanks' rate was reduced to 8 per cent early in 1926—campare the complaints of industrialists in Britain against a 5 per cent. bank rate! The aim of maintaining high rates of interest was to keep prices down, in order to develop an export surplus.

The Dawes Scheme thus involved the maintenance of

railway tariffs, rates of taxation, and rates of interest at a high level at a time when prudent economic statesmanship would have lowered all three. The reason for the conflict between economic statesmanship and the Dawes Scheme is that the former would aim at assisting the German economic system to recover from the weakness and prostration consequent on inflation, whereas the Dawes Scheme aims at drawing the greatest possible tribute without consideration of its effects on the body economic.

Even though its officials are armed with the power to dictate economic policy to the German authorities, however, the Dawes Scheme has shown that it is incapable of getting anything like the sums named out of Germany, because Germany is not capable of producing these sums. If France can only just pay 12½ millions, while for Britain 34 millions is a burden almost too great to be borne, how can Germany pay 60 millions in 1926 and 1927, rising to 87½ in 1928 and to 125 millions in 1929? These figures are fantastically impossible and will have to be revised downward drastically.

The tribute payable by Germany under the Dawes "settlement" is thus quite impracticable; and the mere attempt to extract it, by virtue of atrociously heavy taxation, simply renders Germany unable to compete in world markets, hence unable to develop a surplus of exports, and therefore unable to create any fund from which further payments can be made. What has been paid so far has come almost entirely out of the loan made to Germany for that very purpose. When, in 1927, payments have to be made out of her own production, this disastrous issue of Reparations will again demand attention. Demands made on Germany in the spirit of 1919 to 1923 will threaten once more the stability of the mark and the new equilibrium of Europe.

The alternative to a drastic revision downward of the Dawes payments is to drive far lower the already low standard of living of the German workers. This is the only possible way for Germany to develop a vast export surplus —in so far as other countries' tariffs will allow it. Real wages in Germany are at present [1] lower than they were before the war. Before the war they were lower than the rates then obtaining in England. The only alternative to drastically scaling down the amount of the Dawes annuity is to reduce these low wages still further; to convert Germany permanently, that is, into a coolie plantation paying tribute to Western Europe. Germany would be put into the same position as those villagers of hewers of wood and drawers of water which in the early history of Wales are found tributary to the conquering Celts.[2] How far such an attempt at the permanent ruthless exploitation of a highly-cultured white nation, from which territory and wealth have already been taken on a scale previously unknown in European history, is desirable and likely to be successful is a political question. But it is well that those who call for the payment of the Dawes annuities should face the issue that what they are demanding in fact is one more attack on the standard of living of disarmed German workers.

As regards the debts incurred by the countries allied during the war, the position is as follows: In 1922, when the first debt settlement between Britain and the U.S. was made, Britain owed the U.S. a sum in dollars equivalent, at par, to 978 millions; of this sum 851 millions represented the capital sum borrowed during the war and 127 millions the interest accrued between 1919 and 1922, during which period interest was not paid but added to the principal. Britain in early 1926, up to when no interest had been paid, was owed a larger amount by her former Allies: France was responsible for nearly 700 millions and Italy for about 592 millions; both these amounts include accrued interest. The countries named are further

[1] June, 1926. [2] Seebohm: "Tribal Communities in Wales."

substantially indebted to the U.S. Other "Allies," such as Jugo-Slavia, Poland, Portugal, Rumania, Latvia, Greece, are also indebted to Britain to the total extent of about 100 millions ; and certain of them are also indebted to France.

It should be added that Russia owes Britain about 800 millions, but alleges substantial counterclaims in respect of assistance rendered by Britain to "White" Generals in 1919, and the Russian figures given below are subject to reduction on that account.[1]

Britain thus figures as a debtor to the U.S. and a creditor of the European belligerents, the amount which she was in 1926 entitled to receive being greater, on paper, than that which she was under the obligation to pay.

Britain's original attitude on the whole issue of debts was expressed in the Balfour Note of 1922. The Balfour Note was to the effect that Britain was willing to consider favourably a general writing down of international debts, as between the U.S. and Britain, Britain and her debtors, and the recently allied powers and Germany; but that failing such a general writing down, Britain would be compelled to look to her debtors, including Germany, for settlement to the extent to which she was herself pressed for payment by the U.S. The original British attitude in favour of an all-round cancellation of war-debts was nullified by the refusal of the U.S. to consider such a proposal, and her insistence on payment in accordance with the U.S. Treasury's estimate of the capacity to pay possessed by the various debtors. So far, therefore, as Britain's attitude was concerned, the second proposition contained in the Balfour note became operative, whereby Britain looked to her various "Allied" debtors and Germany to make such payments as together would cover Britain's own payments to the U.S.—the remainder of the

[1] The Russian figures take no account of the destruction and confiscation of the property in Russia of private British nationals, as we are here concerned only with the claims of States against States.

debts, including Reparations owing to Britain, being still regarded as open to cancellation.

The Balfour note thus in effect remitted debt to the extent of the difference between the amount which Britain had borrowed from the U.S. and the amount which she had lent to continental debtors.

In 1922 a settlement was made by Mr. Baldwin on behalf of the British Government with the U.S., whereby the total British debt, including accrued interest, was funded on a basis of a reduced rate of interest, 3 per cent. per annum up to 1933 and 3½ per cent. per annum thereafter, together with a sinking fund of ½ per cent. per annum. This meant that Britain would have to pay annuities, i.e. make annual payments for sixty-two years of about 34 millions per annum up to 1933 and 38 millions thereafter. This is equivalent, as Mr. Churchill illuminatingly put it, to paying £100,000 a day to the U.S. for three generations. Put in another way, it represents 9d. in the pound on the income-tax. Had British claims on her continental debtors been funded on the same terms as her own debt to the U.S., Britain would have received from her debtors a total of 74 to 85 millions per annum, made up as follows:

While Britain was Paying 33 Millions. Million £.		While Britain was Paying 38 Millions. Million £.
23½	France	27
20	Italy	23
3½	Minor Powers	4
27	Russia	31
74		85

The difference between the 33 to 38 millions paid and the 74 to 85 millions received would have accrued to the British Exchequer. As it was, the effect of the Balfour

Note was to remit the difference between 33 and 74 and between 38 and 85, i.e. a matter of 41 rising to 47 millions per annum ; and then to remit a further amount to British "Allied" debtors equal to the amount paid by Germany to Britain by way of Reparations. Assuming the latter to be the 10 millions hoped for, the debt remissions made by the Balfour Note would be 51 to 57 millions per annum.

What this debt remission meant is that Britain, having financed the war partly by disposing of her accumulated wealth (sales of foreign securities) and partly out of taxation, as well as borrowing, while France, Italy, and Russia financed it mainly by borrowing from Britain and the U.S., now agreed to regard a large portion of the debts owed to her as bad and to write off the loss. But as the British State is still responsible to those individuals who had lent it money (War Loans), for paying the interest thereon, and for this purpose it has to tax its citizens, the latter are in effect paying the interest on the money lent to continental "Allies" in place of such interest being paid by the borrowers. The British taxpayer thus took over the cost to Britain of French, Italian, and Russian participation in the war.

Unfortunately for Britain, however, the remissions of debt did not stop there. In 1925 the U.S. granted to Belgium and Italy very much easier terms than those accorded to Britain. The U.S. further offered France substantially more generous terms than those granted to Britain, but these were not accepted by France on the ground that yet easier terms were required. The British Government in 1925, to meet the situation created by the fact that Britain's debtors were negotiating separately with the U.S. in respect of the sums owed by them to the latter, issued the Churchill declaration. This was to the effect that the principles of the Balfour Note still held good, and that Britain expected any arrangements for payment made by British debtors with the U.S. to be accompanied by proportionate and *pari passu* arrangements with ourselves—by arrangements, that is, for debtors in question to pay to us amounts bearing the same ratio to the total amount owed by them to Britain as the ratio of their promised payments to the U.S. bore to their total debt to the U.S.

In 1925 France, in the person of M. Caillaux, made a provisional arrangement with Britain for the payment for sixty-two years of annuities of 12½ millions per annum, subject to this amount being increased if France agreed to pay the U.S. a higher proportion of her debt to the U.S.; but this arrangement was not ratified, and later French negotiations with the U.S. fell through. In the figures given below it is assumed that the agreement with France will be ratified as it stands. Were France to pay Britain in the same proportion as Britain is paying the U.S., her annuity would be 23½ millions per annum up to 1933 and about 27 millions thereafter. Negotiations between Britain and Italy early in 1926 resulted in an agreement whereby Italy pays Britain for sixty-two years a yearly annuity starting with 2 millions in 1926 and rising to 4½ millions, subject to certain modifications of detail. What this meant in the direction of remission of debt is shown by the fact that if Italy had had to pay Britain in the same proportion in which Britain is paying the U.S., Italy would have to pay annuities amounting to 20 millions up to 1933 and thereafter to 23 millions. Satisfactory arrangements with Britain have already been made by Poland, Latvia, Greece, Portugal, and Rumania, and negotiations were, it was understood early in 1926, to be begun shortly by Jugo-Slavia.

Summing up, Britain's attitude originally was that, in default of a general cancellation of war-indebtedness, she desired to receive from Reparations and repayments of debts the amount she has to pay to the U.S., of about 33 and 38 millions per annum. The rest she had forgone absolutely. Even that moderate position was abandoned, not nominally but actually, in the arrangements made. These arrangements provide for a total payment by France and Italy—the other debtors named are negligible—to Britain of 17 millions per annum. The difference between this amount and the 34 and 38 millions payable to the U.S., i.e. 17 and 21 millions, is found by Britain, except in so far as it may be in the future met by contributions from minor debtors and by German Reparations. The former can be estimated, in the opinion of the Chancellor of the Exchequer, at 2 millions; the latter cannot with any great degree of probability be put for the present, so far as Britain's share is concerned, at more than 10 millions. The British taxpayer has therefore not merely remitted to continental debtors—France, Italy, and Russia—the sums above mentioned, but is in addition committed, for two generations, to finding at best 5 millions, and at worst 21 millions, to hand over to the U.S. in respect of money which Britain borrowed from the U.S. during the war in order to lend to France and Italy. He is paying, not merely the cost to Britain of French, Italian, and Russian participation in the war, but also part of the cost to the U.S. of French and Italian participation.

Summing up the settlements in the terms of the British income-tax, the funding of the debts owed to Britain on the same terms as her own debt to the U.S. was funded would mean that Britain, after taking into account her own payments to the U.S., would receive on balance an amount which would enable the British income-tax to be cut by 11d. in the pound. The remissions of debt made to France and Italy mean, assuming that the 1925 arrangements are carried out, that on each of the amounts borrowed by those countries the British income-tax payer will be paying over 5d. in the pound, i.e., after Britain has received from these two countries all that they have promised to pay the British income-tax payer will be paying 11d. in the pound on their joint borrowings, of which the British Government hands over 9d. to the U.S.

In making the various arrangements referred to the principle nominally applied was "capacity to pay," but in fact no scientific ascertainment of capacity to pay was ever made, save in the case of Germany. In the case of France and Italy capacity to pay was estimated by British Treasury experts at about 25 and 8½ millions respectively. These estimates were based on far more moderate ideas of possibilities than those which were accepted by the Dawes Commission in the case of Germany; but, even so, the payments accepted from France and Italy in settlement of their debts, 12½ and 4½ millions respectively, bore no relation whatever to the British Treasury estimates, and represented simply the best offer which could be obtained from the countries in question.

Britain's attitude has thus been extraordinarily generous, unwisely generous, when one remembers the large sums which, since the war, France has lent to her East European Allies for expenditure on armaments. The British income-tax payer, by paying the interest to the U.S. on the French and Italian debts, is, as a matter of actual fact, paying for France's militaristic policy—consider the methods adopted by France on the Rhine, in the Ruhr, in Eastern Europe, Syria, and Morocco—and is subsidizing the competition of French and Italian manufacturers whose tax burden he is bearing.

Yet it is well not to ignore the French point of view in regard to her British and American debts. France says to Britain in effect: "The fact that you are paying the U.S. over 30 millions per annum and receiving nothing from us is your own fault. You should not have rushed in in 1922 and made a settlement with the U.S. without consulting us; we are debtors of both yourselves and the U.S., and the settlement you made has queered our pitch. Had you and we approached the U.S. together we could have got better terms. Your point of view ought to have been identical with ours and opposed to that of the U.S. These debts are not ordinary debts; they were incurred for a common purpose, in which the U.S. themselves shared. They should be reconsidered in the light of the sacrifices made by each one of us for that purpose—sacrifices which were enormous in our case, substantial, doubtless, in yours also (but it would have been for you to argue that); in the case of the U.S. negligible. This is their opportunity to make some sacrifice for what they declared was the cause of civilization and freedom. Furthermore, these debts were incurred when prices were hugely inflated; it would in any case be unfair that they should be repaid in money which is to-day of a purchasing power substantially higher. You have neglected your opportunity and spoiled ours; that is no reason why we should not do the best we can for ourselves."

Such is, in substance, the French case. It is undeniably a strong one, given the political assumptions on which it is based. It would have been infinitely better for Europe, from every point of view, had the original British proposal been accepted: a sponge passed over "Allied" war-debts, and German Reparations drastically scaled down. That it was not accepted was mainly due to the refusal to consider it on the part of the U.S., whose Government has raised the money by taxing or borrowing from its citizens. The U.S. attitude is that the war-debts are to be treated exactly the same as any other debts, and payment of them is to be exacted in full or in any case to the last cent possible. The belligerent nations incurred these debts for their own purposes, with their eyes open, in order to carry out their own policy against Germany; now let them pay for the goods (munitions and food) supplied. From the point of view of a "neutral" country this is a perfectly reasonable attitude; but it is not reconcilable with the professions made by the U.S. when entering the war. If it were in fact a war in defence of justice, civilization, democracy, liberty, etc., then the U.S., whose sacrifices were so small compared with those of France and Britain, ought to welcome the opportunity of sharing a small part of the burden. If, on the other hand, the motives of the U.S. in entering the war were "real" motives dictated by self-interest—the desire of the U.S. Government to protect the rights, real or imaginary, of its citizens, and of the U.S. industrialists to continue their profit-making munition industry at the expense, no longer of the now doubtfully solvent European belligerents, but of the wealthy U.S. Government itself—if such were her motives, then the European belligerents are justified in also doing the best they can for themselves. The U.S. in 1919 properly refrained from making any claim on Germany for Reparations—it is difficult to see what claim she could have made, and she had in any case confiscated the German shipping in U.S. ports—but in fact she is receiving German Reparations through the intermediary of Britain.

The original British proposal of cancellation was wise and far-seeing; her method of dealing with the situation created by the U.S. refusal to consider that proposal was lamentably inadequate. To maintain in its entirety the second of the propositions contained in the Balfour Note it was necessary for Britain to establish a community of action with either the U.S. or with France and Italy. The first course would have rendered it impossible for France and Italy to play off New York against London; the second would have enabled Britain, France, and Italy to present a united front in negotiating with the U.S. In fact, Britain followed neither course. The Baldwin debt settlement was made with the U.S. in 1922, which committed Britain to the payment of annuities of 34 to 38 millions irrespective of whether or not she was paid by her own debtors, to whom this money had been lent; and this settlement contained no provision that Britain should benefit by the easier terms (if any) which might be granted by the U.S. later to her other debtors. In point of fact, far easier terms were granted by the U.S. to Italy and offered to France, but these have not benefited Britain, who continues to pay her 34 millions; and these very settlements made by the U.S. have necessitated Britain making similarly easy settlements with France and Italy and finding the difference out of her own pocket. While French policy has shown its customary skilful adaptation of existing means to immediate practical ends, British policy, far-sighted in its aims, has lamentably failed to safeguard the interests of its people. British statesmanship, in fact, made three blunders in its conduct of this matter. The first was borrowing from the U.S. during the war on behalf of France and Italy, instead of letting them borrow on their own account. But anyone who tried to draw attention to financial matters during the war was denied a hearing. The second blunder was the failure to insist on a debt settlement at the Peace Conference in 1919, where debts should have been made the principal British interest, just as annexation of territory was that of France and her continental allies and the covenant that of President Wilson. The third and most disastrous was the Baldwin settlement of 1922, which committed Britain to paying practically in full without the assurance of receiving anything. It is unfair to blame Mr. Churchill for the generosity of the 1925–1926 offers; all that remained possible after the Baldwin settlement with the U.S. in 1922 was to get as much as France and Italy could be induced to offer. Demands pushed beyond a certain point would simply have been refused, for Britain had no means of enforcing payment. The London money market is not essential to France and Italy; once they made a settlement with the U.S. they could borrow in New York. The time for Britain to have thought of the cost of prolonging the War was when it was a case of negotiating peace. As things are the U.S., if they should scale down war-debts, would benefit Europe by insisting on its equally scaling down Reparations.

As regards the problem of making remittances on a large scale, Britain has so far been able to make such transfers; the Dawes Committee believed that the Agent-General for Reparations would be able to do so; the French wished to make their payments to Britain conditional on the exchange value of the franc remaining unaffected. It is necessary to wait for more experience before we can lay down definitely the conditions under which such transfers can be made without disturbing exchange rates. In the meantime, these international debts constitute a potential threat to the new financial equilibrium. As M. Caillaux put it:[1]

"I say most positively that there will be no economic stability in the world so long as there remains the network of the debts obliging nations to make transfers to other nations. The economic situation of Europe will be at the mercy of any cloudburst. Only one formula can allow us to live: let the sponge be drawn across the slate on which our mutual obligations are inscribed."

The return to gold dealt with in the last chapter may itself be regarded as one of the consequences of the Baldwin debt settlement with the U.S., since that settlement rendered the return to gold not indeed actually necessary, but desirable, for the reasons there given.

The debt settlement and the return to the gold standard are indeed correlated expressions of a rigid adherence to financial orthodoxy as understood in the pre-war period. They show a lack of adaptability to altered conditions which outweighs their evident honesty of purpose. It is a case of trying to solve post-war problems with pre-war ideas. If the currency policy pursued since 1919 seriously aimed at restoring to London her former pre-eminence in

[1] "The Banker," January, 1926.

finance, then it was disastrously misconceived, for the war had definitively ended that pre-eminence. The sudden diminution of Britain's wealth and the increase in that of the U.S. had by 1918 brought to a decisive point and intensified a development which the superior resources of the U.S. would in any case have brought about to a large extent in the course of the century. The war brought the development to a head quickly, by reversing the rôles of Britain and the U.S. as creditor and debtor nations. Before the war Britain was a creditor nation, the U.S. a debtor nation. To-day the positions are reversed. Theoretically, the debts owed to Britain are greater than that owed by her to the U.S. But the U.S.'s debt has been found to be good, and Britain's for the greater part bad; hence the arrangement by which, on balance, Britain is to receive 19 millions (if France pays) plus Reparations per annum and to pay 34 rising to 38 millions.

The reversing of the rôles of Britain and the U.S. as creditor and debtor nations finds expression in the altered position of London in modern international finance. London, from 1918 to 1925, was not a free gold market, whereas New York was: a sterling bill was not, whereas a dollar bill was, a claim to gold which could be always enforced. No occasion has arisen since the war when gold could not be obtained in New York. The change in the conditions of New York compared with the conditions which obtained in 1907 is due to (*a*) the reorganization of the U.S. banking system following 1907 by the institution of the Federal Reserve Bank, and (*b*) the effect of the war in (1) concentrating a large part of the world's available gold supply in New York, and (2) increasing the wealth of the United States and diminishing that of the chief countries in Europe. With the return to gold in 1925, London became again a free gold market, and the other centres named in the foregoing chapter also assumed that position, but the concentration of gold in New York and the impoverishment of Europe caused financial pre-eminence to remain with New York. Theoretically, it might have been expected that the dollar bill would, in international acceptance business of the kind exemplified in Chapter IV, have entirely superseded the sterling bill. In fact, while the vogue of the dollar bill has very greatly increased, the two continue to exist side by side. The reason is that currency factors, like all other economic factors, take time to produce their full effect. Moreover, there are other considerations involved. Custom and prestige play a great part in commerce as in other things. London, having had a long experience of this class of business, knows the ropes in a way that it is quite impossible for New York or any other centre to learn in the course of a few years. New York bankers have frequently been urged since the war to go in more for this class of business, which the financial position of New York renders them eminently able to do, but up to the present they have suffered from the very natural fault of over-caution. They had a big shake-up in the financial crisis in 1907; and, although the U.S. banking system is much securer now than it was then, the conditions of European trade since the war have not been inviting. It is easy to understand the unwillingness which has been evident in New York to extend the credit which is necessary if they are going to do this business. In the post-war state of Europe, and in fact of the whole world, the position of a relatively inexperienced banking community, such as is the New York banking community relatively to that of London, was difficult. London enjoys a predominance in Europe greater than before the war,[1] and it has frequently been the case that payments from continental centres to New York have been made through London. Since things have

[1] The outbreak of the General Strike in Britain in 1926 did not affect the dollar value of sterling, but it sent down the French and Belgian franc, by reason of the apprehension that British bankers would lessen their accommodation, actual or prospective, to those countries.

settled down, however, the international banking and accepting and international banking business of New York has increased steadily, especially in those regions of the world in which America is more particularly interested, i.e. Canada, South America, the Caribbean Sea, and the Far East.

The loss by London of pre-eminence in finance, its connexion with exchange questions, and its results on international trade are excellently illustrated by the following letter which was written in 1920 by the American representative of a firm of cotton brokers in Liverpool to his principals:

"Before the war, Liverpool, as the largest consuming market in the world, set the price, and especially the basis for the sale of cotton to the whole of Europe—that is to say, about seven to eight million bales of American cotton were sold every season, based on Liverpool futures. This was largely due to the fact that London financed all these sales of cotton to continental markets. London was the banking centre of the world, and understood European finance far better than any New York banks. Further, even in America, if a shipper in the South wanted to know what cotton was really worth, he would take the Liverpool prices and calculate from them what he could afford to pay for the purchase of his cotton.

"Since the war this situation has changed entirely. The varying rate of sterling exchange has made it impossible for continental spinners to buy based on Liverpool futures, and now the whole of the business to France, Germany, Italy, Spain, as well as Japan, etc., is all based on New York futures. London is no longer the financial centre of the world, although it is still quite evident that the bankers there understand European financing better than it is understood in New York. Nevertheless, cotton shipped to continental markets is now paid for cash in New York.

Continental spinners, if they now want credit, turn to New York, and not to London, and it still remains to be seen if London will ever be able to regain its financial supremacy."

Since this letter was written, London has again become a free gold market, but cotton is still bought on New York futures: Liverpool, where the buying for the Lancashire cotton industry is concentrated, itself follows New York. That change is permanent.

Another permanent change is that many overseas enterprises and foreign loans which would formerly have been financed in London are now floated in New York.

During the war large quantities of first-class American, Canadian, and South American securities held in Britain were sold in New York—municipal, railway, and public utility bonds, etc. To-day that kind of enterprise in those parts of the world raises its capital in New York. Canadian finance, apart from what is supplied by Canada itself, is almost wholly supplied from New York; similarly in the case of South America. The demands which the undertakings so financed formerly made for sterling in order to pay interest and dividends are now made for dollars, and it is to New York instead of to London that remittances are sent. Equally, it is in Chicago and Detroit, rather than in Birmingham and Glasgow, that the proceeds of these loans are spent.

So far as giving New York the financial primacy of the Western Hemisphere is concerned, the war has hastened by some decades the development which would probably have taken place slowly during the twentieth century. That New York has not so far, however, played the part in financing European reconstruction which was expected early in 1919[1] is due partly to the fact that time is required

[1] This expectation was widely held not only in London but, as the writer can from personal experience testify, in New York as well.

to educate the American investor up to the export of capital, chiefly to the disturbed political conditions of Europe, which involve capital invested in risks which it will not face while safer opportunities obtain elsewhere, e.g., Canada, South America, and the Far East. The existing world primacy of New York, however, is demonstrated by the fact that the main course of money rates in London follows that in New York. Bank rate itself since 1919 has followed the re-discount rate of the Federal Reserve Bank, and the discount houses habitually "watch New York," while sterling exchange is itself protected by a loan from the Federal Reserve Bank.

As the inability to realize what the prolongation of the war has cost Britain is still general in all spheres—witness the constantly heard phrase, "when things get more normal," where "normal" is evidently used as equivalent to "pre-war"—it may be as well to conclude this book by summing up in broad outline the permanent changes which the war has wrought in the exchange world.

(1) The war itself and the political and economic reactions set up by it have destroyed so much wealth that the currencies of all the European nations which took part in it, and to some extent of those which did not, lost value. The means whereby the destruction of values expressed itself in currency values was inflation, but the fundamental cause of the devaluation of the currencies was the destruction alike of wealth, confidence, and credit. (2) As the destruction has taken place in different degrees, the equilibrium of pre-war times has been upset. Hence the currencies not only depreciated in value but also fluctuated wildly. (3) Most of these currencies have now been stabilized, i.e. made exchangeable against gold at fixed rates, but as regards Europe it is only in Britain, Sweden, and Holland that the gold standard has been fully restored in the sense that a free gold market has been re-established. Elsewhere exchange transactions are supervised in one

way or another by the various governments, and, above all, the export of gold is prohibited. The stabilized currencies have remained steady with the exception of the zloty. The French franc has not been stabilized, but could be at any minute so far as financial considerations go; it is political considerations only which keep it unstable. (4) As a result of the stabilization a new financial equilibrium dominated by the U.S. has been set up which is threatened by the factor of international indebtedness—by the fear that the arrangements made may not be carried out—and by the instability of political conditions all over Europe.

The characteristic features which distinguish this new equilibrium from that which obtained before the war are thus (*a*) the absence—apart from New York, London, Amsterdam, Stockholm, and South Africa—of free gold movements, such as existed in the ordinary way before the war; (*b*) the assumption by New York of the pre-eminence formerly enjoyed by London; (*c*) it is, so far as Europe is concerned, an equilibrium between nations subjected to a capital levy disguised as inflation and to unemployment relieved by State assistance: it is, in fact, the equilibrium of a league of impoverished nations; (*d*) it is still menaced by war-debts and rests on political conditions which are everywhere unstable.

The significance of the return to gold in combination with the debt settlement is now evident.

Half the world's gold supply is in New York; New York is the financial centre of the only important creditor nation, which is incomparably richer and possesses incomparably greater resources than any of the other great trading Powers; these Powers are bound to pay to the U.S., directly or indirectly, every year large sums which are measured in gold. Gold before the war was an international currency; to-day it is an American currency. The European nations are, financially speaking, dependent upon and tributary to the United States. That these expressions are not too strong is shown by the part which the United States have played in the politics of Europe and the Far East—a part which would have been simply inconceivable before 1914.

One nation only has avoided this dependence—at a huge cost. Relying on its vast agricultural and mineral resources Russia has turned its back alike on its own traditions since Peter the Great and on European standards generally, and passed out of the West European—and American—orbit.

To ascribe the dependent status of Europe in general and Britain in particular to the return to gold and the debt settlements is correct so far as it goes, but it does not go nearly far enough; the arrangements merely set the seal of formal recognition on the fact of dependence which already existed. There is a twofold mistake to be avoided here: the pound was not freed from its dependence on the dollar by the return to gold, but neither did the return create the dependence. The dependent status existed prior to the return to gold; it was brought about by the impoverishment of Britain, the loss of a substantial portion of the volume of her trade, and by her indebtedness to the U.S. These conditions were the direct results of the war, especially of the prolongation of the war during 1917 and 1918—it was then that the inflation and the impoverishment of Britain's European customers mainly took place and that the American debt was incurred. International finance, like other aspects of the national life of Britain and the various belligerent nations, reveals the decline in national well-being which is the permanent result of the prolonged war. The fact that Britain and France have so far avoided a catastrophe, such as overtook Russia and Germany, obscures the decline, but it does not detract from its significance. France slides down the inflationary slope while Britain watches a declining trade balance and slithers from one industrial crisis to another. The refusal to make a negotiated peace at the end of 1916, as Lord Lansdowne wished to do, affected West European civilization, of which its finance is part, as disastrously as the refusal to end the Peloponnesian War by making "premature peace" wrecked that of the Greeks, and has brought Britain, Germany, and France alike into dependence on the United States. As the Czecho-Slovak journal quoted by M. Caillaux predicted (they see these things more clearly on the Continent): "Europe is about to become a debtor's prison on the highest tower of which will float the star-spangled banner." The world-financial decisions of the future will be made in New York—and ultimately, perhaps, also in Moscow.

BIBLIOGRAPHY

EXCHANGE ARITHMETIC

THOMAS: "Principles and Arithmetic of the Foreign Exchanges."

BILLS OF EXCHANGE

Bills of Exchange Act, 1882.
WHITTAKER: "Foreign Exchange."
SPALDING: "Foreign Exchange and Foreign Bills."

EXCHANGE TRADING

MILLER: "The Foreign Exchange Market."
PHILIPPS: "Modern Foreign Exchange and Foreign Banking."

THE EASTERN EXCHANGES

SPALDING: "Eastern Exchange, Currency, and Finance."
Article in "The Times Trade Supplement" of February 7, 1920.

INTEREST RATES

HARTLEY WITHERS: "Money Changing."
HARTLEY WITHERS: "The Meaning of Money."

INFLATION

RIGHT HON. R. McKENNA: Speech at the Annual Meeting of the Midland Bank, reported in weekly Press of January 31, 1920.
Interim and Final Reports of the Cunliffe Committee (H.M. Stationery Office).
HARTLEY WITHERS: "War-Time Financial Problems" (Chapters III, IV, XVI, XVIII).
PIGOU: "The Political Economy of War."
MORRISON: Article in "The Times Trade Supplement" of May 28, 1921.
CANNAN: Articles in "Manchester Guardian" of January 30 and 31, 1920, entitled "Paper Money and Prices."
CANNAN: "The Paper Pound of 1797 to 1819."
GIBSON: "British Finance During and After the War."

PURCHASING POWER PARITY

KEYNES: "Monetary Reform."
CASSEL: "Money and Foreign Exchange after 1914."
GREGORY: "The Foreign Exchanges Before, During, and After the War."

STABILIZATION

CASSEL: "The World's Monetary Problems."
GREGORY: "The Return to Gold."

INTERNATIONAL INDEBTEDNESS

KEYNES: "The Economic Consequences of the Peace."
KEYNES: "A Revision of the Treaty."

THE PRE-WAR EXCHANGES

GOSCHEN: "The Foreign Exchanges."
HARTLEY WITHERS: "The War and Lombard Street."

INDEX

Printed in Great Britain by Jarrold & Sons Limited Norwich.

For Product Safety Concerns and Information please contact our EU representative GPSR@taylorandfrancis.com Taylor & Francis Verlag GmbH, Kaufingerstraße 24, 80331 München, Germany